HIDDEN TREASURES

MIDDLESEX VOL I

Edited by Lynsey Hawkins

First published in Great Britain in 2002 by
YOUNG WRITERS
Remus House,
Coltsfoot Drive,
Peterborough, PE2 9JX
Telephone (01733) 890066

HB ISBN 0 75433 978 5
SB ISBN 0 75433 979 3

FOREWORD

This year, the Young Writers' Hidden Treasures competition proudly presents a showcase of the best poetic talent from over 72,000 up-and-coming writers nationwide.

Young Writers was established in 1991 and we are still successful, even in today's technologically-led world, in promoting and encouraging the reading and writing of poetry.

The thought, effort, imagination and hard work put into each poem impressed us all, and once again, the task of selecting poems was a difficult one, but nevertheless, an enjoyable experience.

We hope you are as pleased as we are with the final selection and that you and your family continue to be entertained with *Hidden Treasures Middlesex Vol I* for many years to come.

CONTENTS

Daniel Gibson	59
Rayhaan Khan	59
James Cornish	60
Hannah Payne	60
Chelsea Louise Emo	61
Marcus Vining	61
Stephanie Walters	62
Charlie Salisbury	62
Lucie Byles	63
Alexandra McBain	64
Nadine Brenton	65
Andrew Flynn	66
Ashlee Carroll	67
Jordan Haynes	68
Jessica Tovey	68

Deanesfield Primary School

Samantha Hine	68
Gemma Micklewright	69
Samantha Bull	69
Lucy Timbury & Amy Newman	70
Jessica Stewart	70
Michelle Cheung & Jenna Turner	71
Alex Smith	72
Dale Turnbull	72
Laura Latus	73
Rosie Brennan	73
David Baker	74
Monisha Sharma	74
Devon Thwaite	75
Thomas Parker	75
Claire Fyfe	76

Dormers Wells Junior School

Leigh Francis	76
Maaz Khan	77
Davina Johal	77
Bhupinder Gill	78

Chandu Chaudhry	78
Natasha Chapman	79
Nasira Patel	79
Jevanjot Kaur Bhinder	80
Mariam Adesanya	80
Saba Awan	81
Tharindu Fernando	81
Charles Dimitriadis	82

Hampton Junior School

Rebecca Kintoff	82
Lizzie Foster	83
James Birdseye	83
Tom Sheppey, Robert Corr & Sam Imbrey	83
Kiri Poliszewski	84
Anaïs Das Gupta	84
Evangeline Cundle	85
Michael McCubbin	85
Sam Harry Kestenbaum	86
Emily Allen	86
Sebastian Jacques	87
Anna Vere-Bujnowski	87
Sian MacKenzie-Doubleday	88
Sean Lee Rice	88
Sophie Parslow	89
Michael Sheppey	89
Alice Calder	90
George Wilkins	90
Melissa Hampton	91
Michael Plumridge	91
Susanna Hall	92
Harriet Fraser	93
Matty Humphrey	93
Daniel Gale	94
Charlotte Firth	94
Kayleigh Bower	95
Alexander Morris	95

Emily Cheshire	96
Ahad Noor	96
Joseph Allen	97
Georgina Rhoades-Brown	97
Katie Bulford	98
Adam Bartlett	98
Thomas Coggins	99
Daniel Hollands	99
Emily Lavagna	100
Melissa Paris	100
Sarah Carter	100
Adam Amhama	101
Benjamin Pain	101
James Morris	102
Cara Smith	102
Harmanpreet Kaur	103
Caitlin Bartholomew	103
Joseph P Courtley	104
Ella Harding	104
Dominic Paul Futter	105
Nathan Blyth	106
Thomas Headford	106
Shane Nolan	107
Mark Winterburn	107
Tyler Shelmerdine	108
Sally Gardner	108
Annabel Bartlett	109
Raman Jerome	109
Kelly Hardy	109
Lucie Sarah Cassius	110
Jonathan Bestley	110
Hannah Mabb	111
Steven Hall	111
Victoria Brice	112
Hannah Manzur	112
Alice Simmons	113
Jessica Kravetz	113
Oliver Fallows	114

Nicholas Demetriou	180
Daniel Ong	180
Emily Smith	181
Adrian McBride	182
Flora Kupfer	182
Sam Tuchband	183
Molly Campbell	184
William Kupfer	184
Nicole Smallman	185
Reeya Patel	186
Simran Lotay	186
Kanchana Harendran	187

St Ignatius RC Primary School, Sunbury-on-Thames

Kathryn Crockford	187
Stephen Costa	188
Danielle Goody	188
James Crouchman	189
Alexandar Francis-Lynch	189
Max England	190
Danielle Armstrong	190
Chris Bootle	191
Jorja Suchodolska	191
Ryan Frank Hill	192
Rosie Thurgood	192
Holly Thornton	193
Joseph Hood	193
Sophie Ann Perez	194
Jordan Chandramohan	194
Lewis Andrews	195
Daniel Olguin	196
Oscar Finn	196
Emily Harrison	197
Sarah Kane	198
Ciara Reed	198
Naomi Buck	199
Ellie Hill	200
George Standbridge	201

The Poems

THE SILLIEST KNIGHT

The silliest knight is a cowardly knight,
With pants like ants and metal like kettles and a sword
With a cat and a shield made of fields
So he can't possibly win a battle
So he joined a field of cattle.
He was picked for a war so he ran behind a wall.

Danesh Kalia (7)

PLEASE FINISH YOUR HOMEWORK

'Please finish your homework, dear, or no pudding for you.
Think of what you want to do but please finish your homework.
Play with your friends as long as you like but please finish your
                                                    homework
Try to feed the dog without it biting you but please finish your
                                                    homework
Go and do your newspaper round but please finish your homework.'

Gerald Asante (7)
Archdeacon Cambridge's CE Primary School

MY BABY SISTER!

My sister wiggles and giggles.
She's very, very happy except when she has a dirty nappy.
She's nearly 20 weeks with some chubby little cheeks.
She's really very smart
And I love her with my heart.

Ashlea Francis (8)
Archdeacon Cambridge's CE Primary School

THE BIRD OF PREY

The bird of prey glides soundlessly through the air,
The wind blows it towards the sea,
It stays on the cliffs, watching the waves crash on the beach;
There is beauty in the air.

Then the bird, tired of the sea, flies away,
Rests in a tall tree, deep in a forest of pines,
A hunter comes whistling through the wood, a gun on his shoulder;
There is a killer in the air.

He spots the bird and aims his gun,
He shoots at it again, again and again,
Until he finds his mark; the bird gives a sharp gasp
And gradually flutters to the floor;
There is death in the air.

Zack Ellis (10)
Archdeacon Cambridge's CE Primary School

IT WAS BEAUTIFUL

I saw the waves gracefully floating to the shore
And then I saw it,
It had beautiful blue, shiny skin
And it sparkled in the sun.
It leapt up, touching the sun as it went,
It looked as if it was waving at me
And I thought I had known it all the time.
It slowly swam back into the silvery seas
Waving its wet flippers as it swam away.

Gemma McIntyre (10)
Archdeacon Cambridge's CE Primary School

APPLE CRUMBLE

I've loved apple crumble since I was 4
I can't resist the taste
My mum said, 'If there is any spare you can eat it.'

One night I was lying in bed
When I felt an urge for apple crumble
I crept down the landing and
'Oh, oh, oh, oh!'
Have you ever felt the pain of stepping on doll's shoes?
I steadied myself trying not to scream.

I tiptoed downstairs and into the kitchen
I opened the fridge and a dazzling light came out
And out through the light came apple crumble!

I spooned my finger into the crumble
'Mmmmm!' I trickled the sugary flakes into my mouth
Then I got a spoon and dipped the apple treat!
I thought it looked a bit messy so I finished it off
I crept upstairs into my room with a lovely taste in my mouth.

In the morning I got dressed and went downstairs
I got into the kitchen
My mum stared at me
I smiled at her and sat down
Then my mum said,
'Seen any apple crumble around lately?'
I felt uneasy but kept a straight face
'No, not any, unless you have.'
'Well, I can see some on your face.'
'How did that get there?'
I put on an innocent face!

Joy Starkey (10)
Archdeacon Cambridge's CE Primary School

NIGHT FRIGHT!

I am lying awake one night
When I had a terrible fright
I saw something move across the room
Through the very dark gloom.

I jumped out of bed
And bashed my head
I scrambled to the door
Not wanting to touch the floor.

I switched on the light
It was very bright!
I looked round the room
And saw a shadowy figure loom.

Crash! Bash! 'Sugar!' said Chris
'Now get back to bed,' Mummy said.
So it was my brother after all.
I was such a fool.

Emily Dixon (9)
Archdeacon Cambridge's CE Primary School

ICE CREAM

Ice cream, oh ice cream, how lovely it tastes
Vanilla, vanilla, its sweet, sweet taste
Chocolate, chocolate, the smell of it's glorious
Strawberry, strawberry, picked from the fields
Toffee, toffee, how scrumptious it is
Mint, mint, the aroma of Polos
Banana, banana, it comes from Spain,
But my favourite is chocolate, chocolate I eat it every day!

Michael O'Brien (8)
Archdeacon Cambridge's CE Primary School

YUMMY, YUMMY FOR MY TUMMY

Chocolate cake in the dark
In my house in the middle of the park

There it is, small and round
It only cost one pound

But something so cheap
It wouldn't hurt for a little peep!

I put it into my mouth with glee
Let that cake come to me!

The chocolate gobbles down my throat
The choc button on top sails like a boat

It trickles down till it comes to the ground of the basin of my tummy
Mmmmm, that was yummy.

Liam Hicks (9)
Archdeacon Cambridge's CE Primary School

FEAR

My fear is like the evening sky
It tastes like poison
It smells like burnt chicken
It looks like a ghost
It sounds like a high, piercing scream
It feels like my body is broken
My fear is like a goblin
It is shrieks from the darkness
My fear is a lion roaring in the night sky.

Jack Parker (9)
Archdeacon Cambridge's CE Primary School

ORANGE

Round orange, spotty thing,
Just sitting in the fruit bowl
With fantastic, colourful, fruit-like
Apples,
Bananas,
Grapes,
Passion fruits,
Melons,
Mangoes,
Water melons,
Cherries,
Lemons,
Peaches,
Oh, and tomatoes.
Well, back to where we were.
What are those horrid, round, orange, spotty things
Doing with all those other lovely fruits?
I hate oranges.
I hate the way it takes so long to peel them
And the way pith gets stuck in your teeth
But the thing I like about oranges is orange juice!

Rhianne Hannah (10)
Archdeacon Cambridge's CE Primary School

TIGGER TIG TIGER

Tigger Tig Tiger loves running around.
Tigger Tig Tiger loves jumping up and down.
Tigger Tig Tiger loves eating sweets.
Tigger Tig Tiger loves sleeping.
Tigger Tig Tiger loves giving people big hugs.

Emma Bassett (10)
Archdeacon Cambridge's CE Primary School

MY CARAMEL SECRET

When I go to school,
I come back on the bus,
But one Tuesday
I saw a new shop
That had opened up

And one Wednesday
I went in that shop
And saw all these sweets,
Oh such wonderful sweets!

Mints and chocolate,
Boiled sweets in all different shapes,
All the sweets you could ever wish for.
Omm Omm Om . . . delicious . . .

Smacking my lips,
Looking at the liquorice,
But then I saw it,
The lovely bar, up on that shelf.

The most wonderful bar of caramel chocolate,
Just looking at it made my mouth water,
Thinking about the caramel
Sticking to my lips.

Then I bought that bar of
Chocolate and caramel
And gobbled it up in a second
And then no more caramel was left.

When I went home
My mum asked me
What I'd eaten
And I answered, 'Nothing.'

Jaanki Patel (10)
Archdeacon Cambridge's CE Primary School

There's A Tiger In The Kitchen

There was a tiger in the kitchen,
Eating everything,
Eating all our lunch and smashing cups and plates!
There was a tiger in the kitchen,
What should I do, what should I do?
I went downstairs to have a look,
I saw the tiger,
The tiger saw me.
I ran and ran upstairs,
Then into my bedroom.
I jumped into bed and pulled my duvet over my head.
I stayed under my duvet for quite a long time,
But then I got up,
Ran downstairs into the kitchen,
But the tiger was not there.
I looked around,
But the tiger was not there.
I walked up the stairs.
I went into my bedroom.
I got into bed and I though it was all a dream.
But I was wrong.
The tiger had somehow climbed up to my window,
And he winked at me.

Magenta Fox (7)
Archdeacon Cambridge's CE Primary School

Celebrities

They're cool, they rule, they've got the style,
They make watching TV all worthwhile.

They're TV presenters like Ant and Dec,
Or singers and footballers like Posh and Becks.

They've got the attitude, they've got the looks,
Their names go in the record books.

I don't mean to make such a fuss,
But they're more important than any of us.

Zack Fuller (10)
Archdeacon Cambridge's CE Primary School

I Wish, I Wish

I wish, I wish
For a huge house
I wish, I wish
For my sister to turn into a mouse
I wish, I wish
For one million pounds
I wish, I wish
For a shed full of hounds
I wish, I wish
For me never to go to school
I wish, I wish
For my own swimming pool
Oh no, oh no
I can't get a job
Oh no, oh no
I can't look after dogs

So never wish for things
As you don't know what's going to happen
For things that don't seem bad
Can turn out worse!
So I wish, I wish
For everything to
Be normal!

Fenella Pheobe Hawksley-Walker (8)
Archdeacon Cambridge's CE Primary School

MICHAEL, THE SCARED GOALIE

I'm not a good goalie.
Everybody hates me
Because I always let goals in.
I don't want to be the goalie.
I'm just not good.
I don't want to be a goalie.
I don't want to be it anymore.
Each time they shoot, it's a goal.
Why can't I be striker?
I just don't know.
Each time I ask the coach he says,
'No, get back in goal!'
I hate being goalie.
Why can't I just go home?

Jordon Rodney (9)
Archdeacon Cambridge's CE Primary School

MY GOLDFISH RAP

Early in the morning as I get out of bed
I hear a noise as I bang my head
I say, 'Oh please, this is not my day,'
And as I say it, my dad, called Ray,
He says, 'You owe me ten pounds by the way.'
I said, 'Does it look like I care?
I want to know what's under there.'
Oh. you haven't met him yet
He's just Monty, my goldfish *pet!*

Kelly Mackay (8)
Archdeacon Cambridge's CE Primary School

HUMPTY DUMPTY'S MOST FOOLISH FALL

Humpty Dumpty sat on a wall,
Hoping that he would not fall,
He turned around and then eyed,
Up and down, side to side.

A rustle came from far away,
But Humpty Dumpty stayed at bay,
He rose, a club from his side,
He stood up and began to stride.

He wondered if to pull a string,
To make an alarm start to ring,
He had seen a figure that was for sure,
But to act might bring gore.

He was equipped with far too much,
Because when he felt a single touch,
He much too swiftly turned around,
And one second later found,

He was bounding down a hill,
His oval body crushed a daffodil,
He saw a plate that rang a bell,
Of course it was the hospital.

But then he thought what did he touch?
Actually it wasn't much,
Humpty Dumpty must be absurd,
It was only a little bird!

Jeremy Coward (9)
Archdeacon Cambridge's CE Primary School

THE SUN IS THE KING OF THE WORLD

The sun is a spoon of honey dangling over the world.
The moon is a lump of rotten Swiss cheese.
I want to stand on the moon, but it moves around like a gypsy.
The stars are the pictures on my TV.
The planets are my teachers.
The flying saucers are my CDs.
But the sun is the only king of the world.

Ben Gove (9)
Archdeacon Cambridge's CE Primary School

MY MUMMY

She's a nice, cosy bed because she is comfortable and soft
And I can snuggle up to her
In the evening she is the best sunset ever
She is the ripest apple out of them all
She is the snow because she is gentle and playful
She is a newborn puppy because she is sweet and silky.

Natalie Economides (8)
Archdeacon Cambridge's CE Primary School

SHOTGUN

As dangerous as a rhino running at me at rapid speed.
It is a pack of elephants charging at me.
It's as grey as a greyhound.
It feels like I'm trapped in a bullet, suffocating.
Used to destroy without any feelings.
It's like lava burning stuff and destroying everything.

Joshua Faulkner-King (8)
Archdeacon Cambridge's CE Primary School

THE PREDATOR

Sneakily creeping through the grass,
It purrs softly like an engine running low,
Its beautiful fur brushes the grass silently,
It suddenly spots a tiny, little mouse,
Quietly and delicately it picks up a pace,
Sly thoughts slither through its mind,
As it lashes out it scrapes its claw on the mouse,
And the mouse sees the world no more.

Raphaella Carruthers (10)
Archdeacon Cambridge's CE Primary School

STORM

I am the storm! I am the storm!
Crashing, smashing, booming, blasting
I am the storm! I am the storm!
Thundering and roaring
Deadly and pouring
I wreck everything when I pass.

Lydia Fay
Archdeacon Cambridge's CE Primary School

DARKNESS INN

My fingers are trembling,
I know that someone is lurking.
Obviously I am scared.
My clothes are covered in a million creases,
And now I am smashed up into a million pieces.

Ben S Beardon (9)
Archdeacon Cambridge's CE Primary School

AUTUMN LEAVES

I see autumn leaves,
Drift by my window,
Looking at the colours,
Red and gold
I rake them into a pile
And jump into them
So that the dry,
Crispy leaves flutter
In the warm air.
The squirrels are scrambling
In the leaves, birds
Singing in the trees,
Getting ready to fly
Away, leaving their
Nests behind. Those
Sunburnt hands
I used to hold
Since you went
Away, the days
Grow longer, the
Memories of our
Fun day just
Lying in a field
Of gold, eating
Picnics in the
Cool breeze,
In the shade
Eating apples
And slurping
Down our drinks
Thinking of
Our great days.

Abbie Linsey (8)
Archdeacon Cambridge's CE Primary School

THE FASHION

It's in, it's out,
You can shake it all about.

It's up, it's down,
You can wear it in the town.

It's side to side,
It will make you really glide.

It's fashion!

It's in, it's out,
It will make you really shout.

It's up, it's down,
Like a ballroom gown.

It's side to side,
It's never snide.

It's funk, it's punk,
But it's never junk!

Angeline Thushyathan (9)
Archdeacon Cambridge's CE Primary School

HAPPINESS

Happiness is a mass
Of yellow butterflies,
It smells like fresh flowers
And it looks like puppies
Playing in a field.
It sounds like pretty birds singing,
It feels good and you want to smile.

Louisa Browne (8)
Archdeacon Cambridge's CE Primary School

CHELSEA VS WEST HAM

Chelsea Vs West Ham, what a game!
In comes Defoe with a deadly aim
Then comes Hasselbaink with a peck
And hits it past David James' neck
Next comes Unsworth at the edge of the box
After that Defoe slides in with a lucky shot
Which ends up in the middle of the plot
Chelsea thought it was the end of the game
But then they scored again
In extra time, 3 minutes added on
In the second minute Le Saux had a corner
Then in comes Terry and heads in to the top right corner
Wow, what a *game!*

Jonathan Bosier (9)
Archdeacon Cambridge's CE Primary School

TEACHERS

I wonder what teachers do
After the piercing bell strikes 3.15?
The children grab their bags.
The teacher's concentrating, pale eyes
Staring over their pointy, crooked noses.
They walk stiffly around corners, chins in the air.
Creeping past the bakery, the wafting smell of the afternoon air.
Cycling past the grocery.
I think that's what teachers do.

Laura O'Brien (10)
Archdeacon Cambridge's CE Primary School

A SCREAM THAT NOBODY HEARS

Deathly cold.
My torch I hold.
Walking round this prison of darkness.
I flinch.
The stench.
The negative ability of calmness.
The rats scuttle around my feet.
The one little rodent I hate to meet.
It's now and clear.
It's purely made of fear.
The scream that nobody hears.
The slime, it drips.
My foot, it trips.
The sound of people mourning.
The blood, it dries in little pools.
The skin, it shrivels when it cools.
Just red then green then gory!

Jennifer Backhouse (9)
Archdeacon Cambridge's CE Primary School

DAD

My dad is like a bed, all cosy and warm.
He is like 7 o'clock in the morning
Because he always shouts at my sister.
He is prickly like a pineapple
Because he always has prickles on his chin.
He is a sunny day
Because he is always cheerful.
My dad's like a rabbit
Because he always wears soft jumpers.

Amy Pilcher (9)
Archdeacon Cambridge's CE Primary School

THE DOG

Fur, silky and soft.
Teeth shaped like a vampire.
Claws like a bear.
Howls like a wolf.
Eyes glowing like a tiger.
Fast as light.
The dog is a wolf.
It is a cheetah.
Breath stinks like Shrek.
The dog dribbles.
It is a monster.
Wet nose.
Floppy ears.
A sloppy, slimy, floppy tongue.

Charlotte Higgins (10)
Archdeacon Cambridge's CE Primary School

JAKE

There's a boy called Jake,
Who is as thin as a rake.
He whizzed through races and won,
When others had just begun.
He did all his homework on time,
And he made all his big words rhyme.
But one sunny day to his dismay,
He fell down a drain
When it started to rain
And this is the end of my rhyme.
(I hope I've done it in time!)

Rebecca Alexander (8)
Archdeacon Cambridge's CE Primary School

SADNESS

Sadness is a feeling you get,
The tears gather in your eyes,
And it makes you feel really upset,
When other people tell lies.

Sadness won't get you anywhere,
Sadness is horrible,
But you have to take care,
Don't be lonely, be happy.

You feel left out and lonely,
But there's something you forget,
Try to be happy,
And don't be upset.

Emma Duckett (9)
Archdeacon Cambridge's CE Primary School

DADDY

Daddy, Daddy, you're our dad,
And we hope that you'll never be sad,
Because wherever you go you'll be adored by us,
Whether you're in a train, taxi car or bus.
When you kiss us goodnight,
We know we'll sleep tight.
And when we stir up a fight,
You'll tell us to stop and we'll know that you're right.
We are your little girls,
And you'll be with us when our lives unfurl.

Holly Duane (8)
Archdeacon Cambridge's CE Primary School

RICE KRISPIES

I love Rice Krispies
Rice crispies are one of the best snacks in the world,
I remember trying to make a whole plateful once,
Reading the recipe,
Getting all of the things together,
Measuring the right amount.

Crunch, crunch, crunch,
You have to make the toffee smooth,
Get a saucepan,
Turn the cooker down to low,
Put the toffee and some marshmallows in the pan,
And wait for about ten minutes.

Oh, the time went by so quickly,
Now all you do is pour in the Rice Krispies,
And now you have to stir,
Everything is all mixed in,
Now put it I onto a tray and leave to set.

Ohhhh, that is the best,
I can't believe I made it,
Everything is perfect,
But guess what?
I'm not sharing.

Melissa Chin (10)
Archdeacon Cambridge's CE Primary School

MOLLY, MY DOG

She's like a small beanbag
Because she's small and cuddly.
And my dog is like a summer plum
Because she's sweet.

The sun is glittering down with a lovely welcome
Because my dog likes sun.
She's like an eagle
Because she's quick.

Jack Bogalski (8)
Archdeacon Cambridge's CE Primary School

THE DOUGHNUT

You've never tasted a doughnut?
Never bit into the spongy middle?
Never cracked the sweet, sugary skin?
Never even had jam dribbling down your chin?
I'm astounded! I'm flabbergasted!
Tell you what, I'm feeling generous today.
I'll describe what it's like to you.
You walk into the bakery,
Your heart pounding with the suspense.
Your eyes flicker around, searching it out.
Aha! Suddenly you spot it and your heart misses a beat.
You rush to the counter and gibber,
'One jam doughnut with a sticky middle, please.'
You take it home, holding it tenderly, like a baby.
You go to a secret place.
You unwrap it slowly and cautiously.
You nibble a corner. Then another. Then . . .
You scoff it.
You get jam round your dirty lips.
Specks of crystal sugar cover your face.
You munch the spongy, jammy, sticky, gooey,
Browny, sugary, mouth-watering, irresistible
Doughnut.
I wish I had a doughnut every second of the day.

Romy Cowhig (9)
Archdeacon Cambridge's CE Primary School

MARMITE

Mark loves Marmite,
That spicy sauce
That loves to spread.
It goes with butter.
It goes with bread.
It goes with most things
Except for HP sauce.
Mark loves Marmite.
He truly does.

Mark Dennis (10)
Archdeacon Cambridge's CE Primary School

A DOLPHIN

D olphins are soft, dolphins are smooth
O nly one can be the cutest
L ovely
P atient
H elpful
I ntelligent
N o nonsense
S ensible.

Paris Garnett (10)
Archdeacon Cambridge's CE Primary School

FIREWORKS

Flying fireworks
Hazing in the
Sky. Fireworks
Whizz like fire.

It blazes like you
Have never seen
It before. I love
Fireworks.

Florence Williams (8)
Archdeacon Cambridge's CE Primary School

LOVE

Love
It is as red as a heart
It tastes like sugar
It smells like a bed
Of roses
It feels like silk
It sounds like a dove
Flying through the
Air!

Georgina Bonnici (8)
Archdeacon Cambridge's CE Primary School

THE THUNDERSTORM

I am the thunderstorm!
I am the thunderstorm!
Slashing and bashing.
I am the thunderstorm!
Grey and dark clouds,
I devastate lives.

Abigail Pentreath (9)
Archdeacon Cambridge's CE Primary School

SMALL ANIMAL

This is a small animal,
A very small animal,
Not a tall animal.
It gets eaten by moles,
And squashed by people,
(even thought it helps them.)
It lives in a dark, gloomy soil,
And slithers through the grass,
All night, all day,
Day after day,
Night after night.
His name is Worm!

Tom Davies (10)
Archdeacon Cambridge's CE Primary School

WINTER HAIKU

The chilly snowman
In the cold with his coat on
He will melt away

Snowballs are glistening
On my frozen, chilly gate
They will ring all night.

Snowballs are frosty
All through the frosty winter
When children throw them.

Joanna Swan (8)
Archdeacon Cambridge's CE Primary School

CATS

Cats are black, cats are white,
Running round the room all night.
Catching lots of mice all through,
Tripping up people as they go.
They sit on your lap,
They are a good mouse trap.
They sit by your knees saying,
'Can I have some food, please?'

Finuala Optholt (10)
Archdeacon Cambridge's CE Primary School

STARS

As shiny as tinfoil
A row of sparkling dots
It's silver, dust looking
It feels like sharp needles
It's a little light
To guide you through the darkness
Little gems in the blackness.

Lorna Stuart (8)
Archdeacon Cambridge's CE Primary School

THE WEATHER

Rain - drip, drip, drip.
Sun - shining, shining, shining.
Thunder - Bang! Bang! Bang!
Lightning - crash, crash, crash.
Snow - gliding, gliding, gliding.
Ice - sliding, sliding, sliding.

Alice Charlotte Grant (8)
Archdeacon Cambridge's CE Primary School

THE CHOCOLATE CAKE

Chocolate, chocolate, chocolate
Munchy, munch, munch
Crunch, crunch, crunch
Yum, I lick my lips, crunchy
On the bottom, lovely and delicious
My favourite as it melts on my tongue.
Scrumadiddlyumptious, I can taste it already.

Callum Savill (8)
Archdeacon Cambridge's CE Primary School

HATE

My hate is as hot as gas-burnt brown.
It tastes like bitter defeat.
It smells like a monster.
It looks like a curse.
It sounds like a monster.
It feels like I've been shot.

Oliver George (8)
Archdeacon Cambridge's CE Primary School

SNOWFLAKES

Snowflakes drift across the night.
They are very cold,
They melt in my hand.
They are very, very nice to touch.
They mostly come at Christmas time,
But I like them very, very much anyway!

Jade Gutteridge (8)
Archdeacon Cambridge's CE Primary School

EYES

My eyes twinkle and glitter like a starry, bright sky
Over luscious green, fresh-smelling grass.
My eyes are like golden gems on a pitch-black night
Lighting up the world.
My eyes dart around at the speed of light
Like lightning on a stormy, icy, silver night.
My eyes sparkle like fireworks
Blasting-off on a cold night.
My eyes shimmer like icicles that melt on the frosty floor.
Oh, what big, browny, bronze eyes I have.

Rosa Kornfein (9)
Archdeacon Cambridge's CE Primary School

STARE

I am in my bed staring.
I snatch my pear with my pale hand.
I'm still staring.
I hear a noise.
I stare in that direction.
I get out of my bed and stare.
I run downstairs staring.
I stretch my pale hand to my mouth.
I take a bite of my pear.
I step on the cold, kitchen floor.
Boo!

Josh Evans (9)
Archdeacon Cambridge's CE Primary School

MY SISTER

My sister's name is Helen
She is soft and cuddly
Like a fluffy cushion on the sofa.

Helen is like the morning
Because whatever time of day it is
The day has just begun with her.

Helen is like a ripe apple
Because she is kind and helpful.

Helen is like a monkey
Because she is always teasing me.

Robert Miller (8)
Archdeacon Cambridge's CE Primary School

GAMES

The football
Is like a
Big moon
And round
And squidgy
Like a beachball.
We also play
Kickball.
Hockey is rough.
The sticks are tough.
You have had enough
Of games.
Home time!

Stephen Cowley (9)
Archdeacon Cambridge's CE Primary School

BEATINGS

My father beats me up
Just like his father did
And Grandad he was beaten
By Great-Grandad as a kid.

From generation to generation
A poisoned apple passed along
Domestic daily cruelty
No one thinking it was wrong.

And it was:

Not the cursing and the bruising
The frustration and the fear
A normal child can cope with that
It grows easier by the year.

But the ignorance, believing
That the child is somehow owned
Property paid for
Violence condoned.

Sanjeev Dhillon (9)
Ashton House School

BENEATH THE SEA

The light reflects on the sea,
Looking like soft, smooth silk.
It is oh so bright and beautiful,
And the creatures of below dart around like jewels,
Running from their enemies.
'Help!' they cry.

Roma Varma (9)
Ashton House School

A WINTER'S DAY POEM

I walk on the snow that is
Crunching under my feet, it is so cold
That I cannot feel the heat.
When snowflakes hit the hard, deep ground.

When we go outside our noses are cold,
As the snowflakes glitter and fall softy to the ground,
Bells are ringing to celebrate the new year.

The frost is so white and crisp,
It shows its light, glistening brightly,
While footprints are flattened on the ice.

Iman Jasani (7)
Ashton House School

A WINTER'S DAY POEM

I walk on the snow that is crunching under my feet
And I cannot feel the heat
When snowflakes hit the hard, deep ground.

When we go outside our noses are cold
When the snowflakes glitter on Christmas Day
The bells ringing on Santa's sleigh.

When snowballs fly across the sky
While winter white glows so bright
While children look up to see the light.

Neil Mann (7)
Ashton House School

A WINTER'S DAY POEM

On a cold, winter's night,
There is a lovely, sparkling sight,
The streets are full of snow,
The lights inside make a glow.

We are playing, laughing, having fun,
The snow is soft and our work is done!
The snowflakes sprinkle softly,
And the stars glitter in the sky,
Children laugh excitedly,
As the frosty evening passes by.

Nikhita Kripalani (7)
Ashton House School

A WINTER'S DAY POEM

I walk on the snow
That is crunching under my feet
It is so cold
That I cannot feel the heat.

When we go outside
Our noses are cold
As the snowflakes glitter
And fall softy to the ground.
Bells are ringing
To celebrate the new year.

Chloe Alexandria Turner (7)
Ashton House School

THE MONSTERS AND THE KNIGHT

Riding horses through the forest
Defeating ogres all day and night
Bold men fighting with all their might
Battling evil in the rain
Slaying dragons fierce and strong
Monsters dying all the time
The wind is howling through the trees
Brave men running through the cave
Seeing monsters everywhere
Being careful where to step
Trying to escape as he crept.

Munraj Sembhi (9)
Ashton House School

FIREWORKS

F ireworks are the best in town,
I f you miss it, it will frown!
R ocket fireworks lighting the sky,
E ven better that me flying high!
'W ow,' said the people, 'What a sight,
O h, no, my lovely kite!'
R ivers see the patterns in the sky,
K eep the good fireworks high!
S ee what I mean now?

Ishpreet Reel (9)
Ashton House School

THE LIFE OF A SNAIL

A snail goes slowly
And it carries its house
Upon its back
And it leaves a slimy track.
Its face is grey
And its back is brown, slithering around.
A life of a snail is going slow,
But I like snails anyhow.

Taneesha Gadher (9)
Ashton House School

THE MAGIC BOX

I will put in the box
All my troubles and fears,
I will put in the box
All my hopes and careers.

I will put in the box
A wet stream filled with imagination,
I will put in the box
Each and every fret over a situation.

I will put in the box
All the jokes that are funny,
I will put in the box
All the luxury and money.

I will put in the box
Mysteries that do not reveal what happens after,
I will put in the box
Rivers of laughter.

Yasmin Jones-Henry (9)
Buxlow Prep School

My Deepest Thought

I was a little girl of two
Silent yet humorous
I was identical to an angel
But those days were long ago.

Soon life dawned upon me
As sadness did too
A death in the family
I dedicate this poem to you.

My grandfather was the victim
A lovely, perfect man
He trusted other people
Prisoners in jail too
For once they were forgiven
In my grandfather's eyes
They were pure once again.

He was a man of different emotions
A struggling being in Sri Lanka
A smiling person.

I look up to him with respect
Although we never met
I still picture him in my mind
As a man who was so kind.

He is up in Heaven now
Looking down at me
Smiling with great pleasure
Smiling with glee.

He still brings tears to my eyes
As I write the poem
The way I feel now - I cannot describe
But my few words are filled with thoughts that are mine.

Laksha Bala (10)
Buxlow Prep School

THE MAGIC BOX

I will put in the box

An elephant with tusks,
Safe from poachers.

I will put in the box

The dolphins in the great Atlantic
And whales from the Pacific.

I will put in the box

A spoonful of sugar
And shake the box
To make the contents sweeter.

I will put in the box

The people who are cruel to animals and nature.

I will put in the box

Terrorists and tell them to stay in a corner
And taste the sweetness of the box.

I will put in the box

Six sweet candles to lighten my day.

Anushka Trivedi (10)
Buxlow Prep School

THE MIRROR OF MY HEART

Inside the mirror is a whole new world,
Full of joy, happiness and laughter.
There are no wars,
Peace and unity between all nations.

Everyone has food and clean water.
Everyone has housing.
Prisons are few, as the crime rate is low.
No one is inclined to do bad.

Medical care is free.
Treatment for all, rich or poor.
Education standards are high
No one goes without it.

Laws are fair, justice for all.
All races are accepted - no one is judged
Because of their colour or religion.

Everyone lives in unity and respect.
In this world there is love and happiness.
There is hope.

Step out of the mirror . . .

And this amazing place dies.

You're back in a world of hatred.
Murders, drug dealers, terrorists run wild.
Heartbreaking, man-made disasters
That destroy the innocent and bring unrest.

We judge, no one tries to understand each other.
We are surrounded by wars in many parts of the world.
No unity, no love, no respect.
This is the sad world we live in.

But this is my mirror, deep inside my heart.
And what is in this mirror is how I want everything to be.

Alishah Shariff (11)
Buxlow Prep School

A POEM OF TRUTH

A poor man may by wealthy,
In knowledge or wisdom.
A dumb man may be able to speak,
In expression or action.
A blind man may be filled with sight,
In song or praise,
If he looks into the future before him,
And has faith in himself.

A sinned man may be worthy,
In fatherhood or priesthood.
A lame man may be able to walk,
In confidence or positiveness.
A deaf man may be able to hear,
In a sea of paradise or tranquillity,
If he looks into the future before him,
And believes in himself.

For as long as he fills himself
With *hope, kindness* and *love,*
He will survive life's everlasting
Pressures, worries and downfalls.

Lynsey Paul (11)
Buxlow Prep School

THE MAGIC BOX

In the corner of my room there is a box
I can lock away anything.

I can put in gold and silver
The scales of a giant serpent
The teeth of a flying fish.

I can put in the thunder of the sea
The hearts of heroes.

I can put in the box the skeleton of a Jurassic beast
A leopard skin.

The box is as beautiful as the prettiest flower
As small as a Yorkshire terrier.

I can put in the box
All the evil of the world.
All I have to do is put it in and box and *shut!*

George Mizel (9)
Buxlow Prep School

WITHOUT YOU

Without you I'm like
A dragon without fire
A wolf without claws

Without you I'm like
A broomstick without twigs
A game without rules
A crab with no shell.

Barath Nair (8)
Buxlow Prep School

LIFE

There are lots of mysteries,
Among them time - future, histories,
Under the sea and the universe,
The afterlife and man-made curse.
But life is the greatest,
A miracle - not of the latest.
Life is not very clear,
Yet without it we won't be here!
No one knows when life began,
It just blew out like a fan!

Religious says God made life begin,
Some scientist put this reason in the bin.
'It began with a huge, big bang.'
The scientists thought and sang.
Then life they tried to create it
But only succeeded a tiny bit.
They cloned a sheep
But that wasn't very cheap,
They also made a programmed robot,
Life that is definitely not!

Life is trying to have it smooth
Though in life you can have your high and low,
In life there's lots of work to do
And life is also a bit of luck too.
But there is also happiness and joy,
Computer games and having a toy.
In life you relax and have to play
And in an argument have your say.
With all these reasons you have to agree
Life is the greatest, complicated mystery!

James Perera (11)
Buxlow Prep School

THE MAGIC BOX

I will put in the box

The swirl of autumn leaves,
Antlers from great stags,
Diamonds from mines.

I will put in the box

A leaping dive from a curious dolphin,
The sweet juice from a mango,
A crashing tidal wave.

I will put in the box

Sparks from fireworks,
The last gurgle from a baby,
And some butterfly wings.

My box is decorated with diamonds and gold,
With secrets at the bottom,
And dangers on the top,
All tied up with ribbons.

I surf on a tidal wave,
In my magic box,
Then the waves carry me ashore,
To an unknown ancient time.

Maya Gupta (10)
Buxlow Prep School

I WANNA BE A POP STAR

I wanna be a pop star
I wanna have a chocolate bar
I wanna have a lot of fun
I wanna be a shining sun

I wanna be really groovy
I wanna be in a funky movie
I wanna be really famous
I wanna be a pop star!

Katie Hunter (10)
Charville Primary School

THIS IS THE SISTER

This is the sister,
Who pulled my hair,
Who made me scream,
And got my mum.

This is the sister,
Who kept me awake,
Who made me tired,
And made me late.

This is the sister,
Who splashed me in her bath,
Who got me wet,
And got me in trouble.

This is the sister,
Who pinched my cheek,
Who made me weep,
Then kissed me, isn't she sweet?

This is the sister,
Who pulled my hair,
Who kept me awake,
Who splashed me and got me wet,
Who pinched my cheek,
This is the sister who is trying to speak.

Abby Elliott-Gay (9)
Charville Primary School

THIS IS THE HORSE

This is the horse
Who bucked me off
Who broke my leg
And made it hurt.

This is the horse
Who made me win
Who made me smile
And the crowd cheered.

This is the horse
Who stepped on my toe
Who made me cry
And hobble home.

This is the horse
Who gave me a lick
Who nuzzled me close
And made me feel warm.

This is the horse
Who gave me a lick,
Who made me cry,
Who made me win,
Who broke my leg,
This is the horse
That I love.

Amy Youngman (9)
Charville Primary School

TIME TO WAKE UP

Crash, clatter,
My feet on the floor,
Swoosh, smoosh,
Brush my teeth.

Drip, drap,
Milk in my bowl,
Crunch, munch,
Eat my breakfast.

Harry James Coysh (9)
Charville Primary School

THIS IS MY DOG

This is my dog,
Who barks when the bell goes,
Who sits when he's told,
And likes going for walks.

This is my dog,
Who eats very loudly,
Who likes the rain,
And who is very stupid.

This is my dog,
Who looks very sad,
Who licks me when I'm upset,
And gives me big hugs.

This is my dog,
Who likes the sea,
Who likes the beach,
And likes to play ball.

This is my dog,
Who likes the sea,
Who looks very sad,
Who eats very loudly
And who barks when the bell goes.

Georgia Harris (9)
Charville Primary School

THE ROOM

This is the room where the bed collapsed
Cos my sister got on it
And that was that

This is the room where the wardrobe collapsed
Cos it had so many clothes in
And that was that

This is the room where the carpet got ripped up
And fell through the floor
And that was that

This is the room
Where the bed collapsed,
The wardrobe broke down,
The carpet fell in . . .
And that was that.

Lauren Thorpe (9)
Charville Primary School

THE GORILLA

A two tonne giant
Moving across the jungle.
An aeroplane, fast but quiet.
Loud as thunder mouth.
His black, gutter arms
Hit his drum chest
As his football feet
Stumble along the floor.
His nose, a lump of clay
Sniffing along the floor
For food.

Charlie Marskell (9)
Charville Primary School

This Is The Room Where . . .

This is the room where,
I was born,
My mother was sad
And I cried.

This is the room where,
I rolled over,
Hit my knee
And cracked my head open.

This is the room where,
My mum sleeps,
My brother first talked
And my sister got married.

This is the room where,
All these wonderful, sad, happy
And confusing things happened.

Kadra Aden (10)
Charville Primary School

I Wanna Be A Tennis Player

I wanna be a tennis player
I wanna see the prince and mayor
I wanna be the best of all
I wanna own lots of tennis balls
I wanna have a flashy car
I wanna see the moon and star
I wanna hit the ball to space
I wanna get a super ace
I wanna be a tennis player!

Kemi Akingbade (10)
Charville Primary School

THIS IS THE DAD

This is the dad
Who took me to America
And took me snowboarding
Up in the mountains.

This is the dad
Who took me to football
And bought me a hot dog
And kept me warm.

This is the dad
Who makes the dough
Spends it on me
Don't you know.

This is the dad
Who's big and cuddly
It would take ten of me
To circle his waist.

This is the dad
Who likes to have fun
The problem is
He weighs a tonne.

This is the dad
Who took me to America
Who took me to football
Who makes the dough
Who's big and cuddly
Who likes to have fun
This is the dad
Who loves me always.

Ben Scott (10)
Charville Primary School

I WANNA BE A POP STAR

I wanna be a pop star.
I wanna drive a flashy car.
I wanna be a pretty star.
I wanna be the best to sing.
I wanna be a pop star.
I wanna be funky at night.
I wanna get everything right.
I wanna go to see the moon.
I wanna see it very soon.
I wanna go up very far.
I wanna be a pop star.
I wanna go round in a limo.
I wanna wave out of my window.
I wanna eat all the grub.
I wanna be a pop star.

Kirstie Edwards (10)
Charville Primary School

THE HAMSTER

The hamster is a slow mover,
It is also small and furry,
It has sharp claws and big, sharp teeth,
It lives in a cage,
Hamsters can be any colour,
It has small eyes and nose,
It is like a very, very small cat,
It is as soft as a pillow,
It is as furry as a bird,
They've got a tiny tail,
Like half the size of my little finger.

Danielle Deacon (10)
Charville Primary School

MY CAT

This is the cat,
Who clawed my lap,
Who tore my shorts,
Who ate my fish.

This is the cat,
Who sat on my lap,
Who purred at me,
Who licked my ear.

This is the cat,
Who bit my finger,
Who ate my homework,
Who scratched my sister.

This is the cat,
Who clawed my lap,
Who licked my ear,
Who ate my homework,
This is the cat that I love.

Georgia Butcher (10)
Charville Primary School

AN ART LESSON

Splat, flat
Right on the mat
Clitter, clatter
Table jibber jabber.

Smash, clash
The pot of paint - splat
Screech, scratch
Tuck in my chair.

Bomb, domb
I drop my brush
Quickly, quickly
I'm in such a rush.

Stomp, stomp
Well all run out
'Waa hooo!'
We all *shout!*

Lucy Newman (9)
Charville Primary School

ART LESSON

Creak, scratch
Tuck in my chair
Splish, splash
Paint everywhere

Scratch, scratch
Teacher moans
Splitter, splatter
Children groan

Squeeze, squirt
Some on the candle
Squish, squash
Now it's on the handle

Screech, crash
Paint on the floor
Bang, crash
Some on the door.

Kamaljit Dhaliwal (10)
Charville Primary School

I Wanna Be A Golfing Star

I wanna be a golfing star.
I wanna drive a really fast car.
I wanna be the best of them all.
I wanna play football in the school hall.
I wanna have a pet rat.
I wanna have a Tiger Woods' mat.
I wanna hit a golf ball far.
I wanna be a golfing star.
I wanna go on a golf course.
I wanna ride a really fast horse.
I wanna be a golfing hero.
I wanna get the ball in in zero.
I wanna have brand new clubs.
I wanna be a golfing star!

Ross Thompson (10)
Charville Primary School

The Shark

There you are,
Swimming forever and ever,
A stealthy submarine,
Gliding through the water like you are flying.
You slither and slide almost unnoticed,
You make no sound,
Just like you have lost your voice box
But certainly not your appetite.
You can slowly sloop through the water
Or swiftly shoot so no one can see you.
Either way you are ready to jump into action
At the slightest disturbance in the water.

Harry Manners (10)
Charville Primary School

I WANNA

I wanna be a pop star.
I wanna drive a massive car.
I wanna be a famous singer.
I wanna be a millionaire.
I wanna have the nicest hair.
I wanna sing in that microphone.
I wanna have the biggest comb.
I wanna be a pop star.
I wanna have a flash guitar.
I wanna have lots of fun.
I wanna fly up to the sun.
I wanna stay up at night.
I wanna have a flying kite.
I wanna, I wanna, I wanna be a pop star!

Ellie-Rose Park (9)
Charville Primary School

THE LION

The lion is a hairy, yellow monster
It jumps like a kangaroo
It moves like a hunter
It runs fast when it hunts something down.
The lion's skin colour blends in the golden sand
The river he drinks from is as sparkled as spring.
The way he looks like is a hairy animal
It looks like a puppy when it's young.
It makes a frightening sound like a scary movie
It makes a rough sound.
The lion jumps over rocks and logs
His skin blends in the golden, shiny paint.

Paramuir Singh Choat (9)
Charville Primary School

THIS IS THE BROTHER

This is the brother,
Who threw a strop,
Who smashed a window,
And laughed and laughed.

This is the brother,
Who shared his toys,
Who made me laugh,
And made me smile.

This is the brother,
Who said, 'You're the best,'
Who gave me his sweets,
And said, 'You're a good friend.'

This is the brother,
Who shouts and screams,
Who calls me names,
And gives me support.

This is the brother,
Who laughed and laughed,
Who made me smile,
Who said, 'You're my friend,'
Who gives me support,
This is the brother,
That I wouldn't swap for all the world.

Jordan Day (10)
Charville Primary School

I WANNA BE A POP STAR

I wanna be a pop star
I wanna drive a funky car
I wanna be like Kylie
I wanna get paid highly

I wanna have some fun at night
I wanna see all the lights
I wanna be number 1
I wanna be a pop star!

Leah Baker (9)
Charville Primary School

THIS IS THE TEACHER

This is the teacher,
Who lost all the kids,
One over here,
One over there.

This is the teacher,
Who lost all the books,
One over here,
One over there.

This is the teacher,
Who likes us on time,
Who gets us in line,
And then leads us one at a time.

This is the teacher,
Who gets in a state,
Who keeps us in late,
So at the end of the day we run to the gate.

This is the teacher,
Who keeps us in late,
Who gets us in line,
Who loses all the books,
This is the teacher,
Who lost all the kids.

Chelsea Small (9)
Charville Primary School

THIS IS THE ROOM

This is the room
That is full of disaster
So if you go in
You'll never come out.

This is the room
Where the bed collapsed
Made me jump
And made a crash.

This is the room
Where we play
There's lots of toys
For girls and boys.

This is the room
That is always a mess
Nothing ever fits
Because of the mess.

This is the room
Where nothing ever fits,
Where we play,
Where the bed collapsed,
Which is full of disaster,
This is the room
That I love.

Daisy Abbott (10)
Charville Primary School

MY FOOT

This is the foot
That touched a ball
That scored a goal
That ran into the pole

This is the foot
That went to a disco
That had a dance
That went to France

This is the foot
That went in the woods
That saw a frog
That tripped over a log

This is the foot
That went in the bath
That lost the soap
That couldn't float

This is the foot
That lost the soap,
That saw a frog,
That had a dance,
That scored a goal,
This is the foot
That never gets lost.

Joe Shepherd (10)
Charville Primary School

THE SEAGULL

The seagull
You can fly with them,
Walk with them,
Even swim with them.

The seagull
You can play with them,
Talk to them,
And play in the sand with them.

The seagull
You won't do a lot in the end,
But it might plop on you,
One day it will drop
And thank you!

The seagull
You can walk with them,
Talk to them,
You won't do a lot in the end.

Harley Thorne (9)
Charville Primary School

THE SHARK

There I swim
In the middle of the sea
Staring at my prey
With my deadly teeth
Like knives
Going through your skin
And I will kill you.

Simon Coffey (10)
Charville Primary School

THIS IS MY DAD

This is my dad
That does all the cooking
That makes everything nice
Especially rice

This is my dad
Who likes fast cars
One day he hopes
He will have a Lambourghini

This is my dad
Who still plays football,
He likes to score goals
But misses and hits the pole

This is my dad
That does all the cooking,
Who likes fast cars,
Who still plays football,
I think he's the best dad.

Charlotte Ponsonby (10)
Charville Primary School

PIRANHA

There you lurk
Buried in mud
An armed torpedo
In the murky river
You move swiftly
Like a submarine
Often going upstream.

Tom Salter (10)
Charville Primary School

I WANNA BE

I wanna be a pop star
I wanna drive a groovy car
I wanna win the lottery
I wanna buy some pottery
I wanna be a superstar
I wanna work behind a bar.

I wanna be famous
I wanna drive a fancy car
I wanna be so famous
I wanna be a groovy star
I wanna be a number one
I wanna be lots of fun
I wanna be a pop star!

Holli Johnson (10)
Charville Primary School

I WANNA BE A POP STAR

I wanna be a pop star
I wanna have my own bar
I wanna have a lotta fun
I wanna be the fastest run
I wanna have the perfect hat
I wanna have a tabby cat
I wanna have an expensive flat
I wanna have another cat
I wanna travel so far
I wanna be a pop star!

Rosie Cathryn Ganna (10)
Charville Primary School

I WANNA!

I wanna be a pop star
I wanna go really far

I wanna stay up at night
I wanna have a massive fight

I wanna be no 1
I wanna have lots of fun

I wanna meet Posh and Becks
I wanna dance with Ant and Dec

I wanna be a pop star
I wanna, I wanna, I wanna be a pop star!

Daniel Gibson (10)
Charville Primary School

I WANNA BE A POP STAR

I wanna be a pop star.
I wanna drive a super car.
I wanna see the lovely star.
I wanna own a neat bar.
I wanna be really rich.
I wanna have a big football pitch.
I wanna be a pop star.
I wanna have a huge house.
I wanna have a funky mouse.
I wanna join a pop group.
I wanna have a handsome hoop.
I wanna be a pop star!

Rayhaan Khan (9)
Charville Primary School

THE SHARK

An enormous killing submarine,
A grey beast gliding through the sea,
It is a monster of destruction,
It is as sly as a thief.

Stealthily moving through the water,
Its fin is as sharp as a blade,
It swims from coral to coral, nearer to its prey,
It is a munching, crushing vehicle.

It will eat anything in its path,
Swooping silently through the sea,
The monster of the world is out there,
It is the king of the water.

Jaws the size of mountains,
Don't mess with the devil of the water.
Don't go in the sea,
Or it will come for you.

James Cornish (10)
Charville Primary School

BUTTERFLY

There you fly
Gliding through the sky
Fluttering gently on the wind
Hovering over the flowers
In the summer sunshine
With your colourful wings.

Hannah Payne (10)
Charville Primary School

THE STARFISH

My little starfish lay there like a star dreaming
It was like a bumpy road
And all squashy like a piece of jelly
And wobbles all day long
It's like a burning sun
It's bright, sparkling orange
It's like a tiny ant
It's so small you can't see her
Plus it's very cute
It's got a bit of bute
It's very dotty
It's like she's got chickenpox
It slivers round like a snail
Her friends are all different sizes
One of her friends is different
Some are light
Some have different heights.

Chelsea Louise Emo (9)
Charville Primary School

THE LION

There you lie,
Laying on the grass.
An armed man,
In your jungle camouflage.
You stay silent,
Like an army man,
Pouncing on his prey.

Marcus Vining (9)
Charville Primary School

Rappy Bend!

When you're down in the dumps and feeling sad
Remember your mum and remember your dad.
Don't let them make you all stressed and hot
Even when you ain't got a lot.

Auhur werhoo,
Auhur werhoo.

When you're down in the dumps and have nothing to do
Feeling cold and lips are blue
Come back soon 'cause this is the end
So stay tuned to the Rappy Bend!

Stephanie Walters (10)
Charville Primary School

I Wanna Be A Pop Star

I wanna be a *pop star*
I wanna, I wanna, I wanna be famous
I wanna song for number six
I wanna eat a Twix
I wanna be a *pop star*
I wanna have lots of fun
I wanna be in the paper
I wanna have lots of red
I wanna friend called Fred
I wanna be on TV too
I wanna be a *pop star!*

Charlie Salisbury (9)
Charville Primary School

THIS IS THE MOUTH

This is the mouth
That whispers and shouts
Sometimes it kisses
And sometimes it misses

This is the mouth
That wears lipstick all day
Red and mauve and pink and blue
It sticks a lot just like glue

This is the mouth
That shivers when cold
This happened every day
But always goes away

This is the mouth
That eats loads of food
Cereal and chips and potatoes and meat
Everything goes down a treat

This is the mouth
That eats loads of food,
That shivers when cold,
That wears lipstick all day,
That whispers and shouts,
This is the mouth
That sings on the roundabouts.

Lucie Byles (10)
Charville Primary School

THIS IS THE MOUTH

This is the mouth
That went on stage
That sang a song
And made my tongue long.

This is the mouth
That went in the kitchen
That ate a crumb
And bit the thumb.

This is the mouth
That went to school
That said its fables
And its times tables.

This is the mouth
That yelled so loud
That got a sore throat
So now it can only croak.

This is the mouth
That yelled so loud,
That went to school,
That went in the kitchen,
That went on stage,
This is the mouth
That never gets lost.

Alexandra McBain (10)
Charville Primary School

THIS IS THE FOOT

This is the foot
That spends lots of money
That loves to shop
But will never drop

This is the foot
That squashed a banana
That made it fly
High in the sky

This is the foot
That goes to the pub
That has lots of wine
And says 'They are all mine!'

This is the foot
That's never tied
That has to count sheep
To get to sleep

This is the foot
That's never tired,
That goes to the pub,
That squashed a banana,
That loves to shop,
This is the foot
That is a real hoot!

Nadine Brenton (10)
Charville Primary School

THIS IS THE FOOT!

This is the foot
That kicked the ball
Went into the goal
And hit the mole

This is the foot
That passed to a dad
That was on the pitch
Who kicked it into the ditch

This is the foot
That hit the ball
Hit the bar
And bashed a car

This is the foot
That wears a boot
That goes in goal
And his friend plays like Andy Cole

This is the foot
That wears a boot,
That hit the ball,
That passed to a dad,
That kicked the ball,
This is the foot
That got lost.

Andrew Flynn (10)
Charville Primary School

THIS IS THE FOOT

This is the foot
That touched my shoe
That touched the ground
And made a sound

This is the foot
That touched the carpet
That was so fluffy
And made it red

This is the foot
That touched the bath
That tickled my toe
And made me laugh

This is the foot
That took me to bed
Where I lay down
My sleepy head

This is the foot
That took me to bed,
That touched the bath,
That touched the carpet,
That touched my shoe,
This is the foot
That took me to the loo.

Ashlee Carroll (9)
Charville Primary School

I WANNA BE A POP STAR

I wanna be a pop star
I wanna have a fancy car
I wanna have a heavy pet
I wanna drive a big jet
I wanna, I wanna be a pop star!
I wanna drive really far in my little, fancy car
I wanna own a private bar
I wanna be a pop star!

Jordan Haynes (9)
Charville Primary School

ART LESSON

Splish, splash
The water comes out of the jug.
Ding dong
The paint is on the paper.
Swish, swash
With the paint brush.

Jessica Tovey (9)
Charville Primary School

SADNESS

Its colour is blue,
It feels like a cold shiver shooting down your spine,
It smells like rotting wood,
It lives in the heart of every teardrop
That eventually falls to the ground,
It tastes like salty water.

Samantha Hine (9)
Deanesfield Primary School

IF I WAS GROWN UP

If I was grown up I'd climb a mountain,
If I was grown up I'd swim the sea blue,
If I was grown up I'd write by a fountain,
But that surely won't happen, it's true.

If I was grown up I'd go my own way,
If I was grown up I'd be carving wood,
If I was grown up I'd laze all day,
There's no point in thinking, it's no good.

I like being a kid,
It's better for me,
I don't have to bid,
So tell me I'm free.

Gemma Micklewright (9)
Deanesfield Primary School

MY MIND

The rain hurries down, glistening,
Falls down gently, flowing fast,
Trickling, running rapidly,
Through scars of lonely forest.

My mind runs like a river,
With mind swirls of blue and black,
Colours twisting and twirling,
Lightning set free from the clouds.

But a stream comes running down,
To a sea of endless thought,
Turquoise in tranquil waters,
Set free in the open sea.

Samantha Bull (10)
Deanesfield Primary School

SPRING, SUMMER, AUTUMN, WINTER

Tranquil birdsong, like a lullaby hushing a baby to sleep.
Newborn animals take their first look at the world timidly.
In their first few days of life feeble birds are assimilating how to fly.
Demure sunrays start to peep through.

The heat is too exhilarating for some.
The sunrays shine pertly down on the meadows.
Summer holidays stimulate the tired mind.
Breathtaking sunsets loom over the Earth.

The glum look is the latest fashion as children return to school.
Perilously the wind blows down fences and uproots trees.
The days go by tediously like a tractor plodding along.
Dishevelled trees whimper at the thought of a gust of wind.

The gales are ponderous like the beat of a drum.
Jack Frost frigidly coats the gardens in thick frost.
Children trek sluggishly through the snow with their boots caked in
mud and snow
Muscular ice clings to rivers, lakes and ponds.

Lucy Timbury (10) & Amy Newman (11)
Deanesfield Primary School

LOLLIPOP

Lollipop, lollipop, ceiling to floor,
Lollipop, lollipop, flavours galore,
Lollipop, lollipop, always want more . . .
But shopkeeper won't let me through the door.

Lollipop, lollipop, can't you see?
Lollipop, lollipop, we're meant to be,
Lollipop, lollipop, it's you and me . . .
But shopkeeper leaves me by a tree.

Lollipop! Lollipop! Ceiling to floor!
Lollipop! Lollipop! Flavours galore!
Lollipop! Lollipop! Always want more . . .
Oh stuff it, I'll just go home!

Jessica Stewart (10)
Deanesfield Primary School

FOUR SEASONS

Spring
Fresh, new grass pushes through soft soil,
Budding flowers scent the air,
Blossom buds appear silently on young trees,
Soft petals fill gardens with colour.

Summer
Thick green leaves cover brittle bare branches,
Rich, green grass creates a delightful scene,
Flowers grow bright and beautiful,
A strong, blazing sun shines its tangible rays.

Autumn
Ghastly gales set a dull atmosphere,
Rain shoots across the window like shooting stars,
Gloomy clouds hide the sky like patchwork,
Withered leaves are snatched up by forceful winds.

Winter
Soft snow rests upon a tired world,
Bare trees look dull and gloomy,
Icy chills whip past,
Frost sparkles in the glittering moonlight.

Michelle Cheung & Jenna Turner (10)
Deanesfield Primary School

SEASONS

I'm the birth of the relaxing birdsong which young and old adore.
I make flowers bloom exuberantly with a calming scent.
I give people a new start in life, turning over a new leaf.
I make people feel fabulous, it's almost tangible.

I am the maker of magnificent sunsets that glisten in the sparkling sea.
I have blazing rays which hang like a necklace from the powerful sun.
I make the calm sea shimmer by the ridged cliffs.
I make happiness float through the stunning beaches.

I am the loathe of the year, I rip the skin off trees with my roaring
winds
I shred the naked trees of their crisp leaves.
I make atrocious storms which rip and tear.
I slam doors and destroy fences with my thoughts.

I make ice crack with anger and snow fall violently.
I kill and destroy everything in my path.
I freeze and dismantle anything in the way.
I make things sleep forever.

Alex Smith (10)
Deanesfield Primary School

SILENTLY, SOFTLY

Silently, the leaves fall from the tree like a swooping bird
Softly, my baby brother jumps up and down on my bed like a rabbit
Silently, butterflies fly around all day long
Softly, the rain pelts down
Silently, a bird flies around all day landing on cables and roofs
Softly, the chalk scrapes on the blackboard
Silently, the children work.

Dale Turnbull (10)
Deanesfield Primary School

DAYDREAMING IN MATHS

I'm in maths, daydreaming,
I'm now a pop star singing in front of a crowd.

I'm still in maths but looking out of the window,
I'm the world's fastest runner speeding along the track.

I'm gazing at Miss I M Boring blabbing on,
I'm now a famous writer scribbling on a notepad.

I'm doing a maths test,
But now I'm the Prime Minister running England.

I'm now back to Earth,
Back to real life
Because I'm none of that,
I'm just *Laura!*

Laura Latus (9)
Deanesfield Primary School

THE GLOOMY SHADOW

The raindrops were transparent stones hammering against the glass,
And the wind was a gushing of leaves skipping through the grass.

I looked out of the polka dot window to see what would be there,
And then I saw a shadow with a gloomy-looking stare.

I put my eyes in focus to prove what I could see,
And then I finally realised the shadow belonged to me.

Rosie Brennan (10)
Deanesfield Primary School

VICTORY/DEFEAT

Victory is crystal clear white.
Victory smells like beautiful, blossomed flowers.
Victory tastes like a delicious, cool glass of orange juice.
Victory sounds like the fans chanting for their champion.
Victory feels like the cushioned surface of a lion's mane.
Victory lives in the memory of everyone around the world.

Defeat is bloodshed red.
Defeat smells like molten rock beneath the Earth's core.
Defeat tastes, like burning lava making its way out of the Earth's
surface.
Defeat sounds like dragons raging through the land.
Defeat feels like a stab of a sword going through his soul.
Defeat lives in the deep darkness of a man's soul.

David Baker (10)
Deanesfield Primary School

LOVE AND HATE

Love is red like a juicy strawberry,
Love tastes sweet and sugary,
Love sounds like trickly rain,
Love feels like a soft, fluffy cushion,
Love lives in the heart of a human.

Hate is black like burning coal,
Hate tastes like poison on a piece of apple,
Hate sounds like a nail being scraped on a blackboard,
Hate feels rigid and sharp,
Hate lives in the Devil's voice.

Monisha Sharma (11)
Deanesfield Primary School

LOVE AND HATE

Love is pink like a rose's head.
Love smells as sweet as a scent of a baby.
Love tastes like sugar that tickles your tongue.
Love sounds like a high-pitched triangle.
Love feels smooth like your skin.
Love lives in the seaside where it's warm and relaxing.

Hate is black like coal.
Hate smells deep like a can of petrol.
Hate tastes like a bitter apple.
Hate sounds like a drum which gets louder and louder.
Hate feels prickly like a sharp thorn.
Hate lives in a dark place where it can't be let out.

Devon Thwaite (10)
Deanesfield Primary School

LIFE AND DEATH

Life is white as white as a cloud.
Life smells like perfume from a bottle.
Life tastes like sweet juice from an orange.
Life sounds like children singing merrily.
Life feels like a nice, fluffy pillow.
Life lives in the heart of the heavens.

Death is as red as lava from a volcano.
Death smells like a fire that's been put out.
Death tastes like an eyeball from an animal.
Death sounds like people screaming with terror.
Death feels like a human's skull.
Death lives in the heart of the Devil.

Thomas Parker (10)
Deanesfield Primary School

LOVE

Love is red,
It smells like roses,
Love tastes like fresh oranges,
It sounds like the beach at night,
It feels soft and shiny,
Love lives in my heart forever and ever.

Claire Fyfe (10)
Deanesfield Primary School

DORMERS WELLS JUNIOR

D   is for Dormers Wells
O   is for orange juice
R   is for RE
M   is for Mrs or Miss
E   is for English
R   is for reading
S   is for silence

W   is for wicked school
E   is for everyone I meet
L   is for Leigh, that's me
L   is for light we have in our class
S   is for science.

J   is for junior school
U   is for umbrellas we bring on rainy days
N   is for nice people
I   is for ice cream
O   is for oranges we have at play
R   is for our reading groups.

Leigh Francis (10)
Dormers Wells Junior School

HALLOWE'EN

It is the October the thirty-first,
It is the month of the worst.
We dress in costumes and a mask,
Scaring all the kids is our task.

Pumpkins, cauldron and a witch's broom,
It is time for children to meet their doom.
We collect candy and lots of money,
Scaring everyone is extremely funny.

I love to dress up as a ghoul,
Jump around and play the fool.
1st of November is drawing near,
The ghouls and goblins will soon disappear.

Maaz Khan (11)
Dormers Wells Junior School

PLAY TIME AT MY SCHOOL

It's play time at my school
Play time is very cruel
People being very mean
Right outside the school canteen

Bullies shouting, 'Give your money,'
People don't think it's very funny
Teachers yelling, 'Go away,'
Headmaster screaming, 'Go and play.'

Shouting, playing games on the yard
Making friends is very hard
I love Year 6, it is the best
We're working towards our SATs tests.

Davina Johal (11)
Dormers Wells Junior School

SCHOOL

My new school is really fab,
All the teachers are great.
Sports, literacy and the science lab,
For lessons I'm never late.

My favourite subject is English,
I think maths is really boring.
In English I can write what I wish,
Numbers and sums always have me yawning.

School has lots of rules,
To keep us safe and sound.
Some children can be really cruel,
It's good we've got teachers around.

Year 6 is the best,
We prepare for high school.
Working towards our tests,
I think high school will be really cool.

Bhupinder Gill (11)
Dormers Wells Junior School

THE BUSY BEE

I'm busy in the flowers
And I'm busy in the trees
I'm such a busy body
I'm such a busy bee
I'm busy making honey
And I'm buzzing busily
I'm busy being busy
I am a busy bee.

Chandu Chaudhry (10)
Dormers Wells Junior School

THE DEER

The deer prances over and over
The soft, turf-filled hills of green,
As he prances over, happiness is what he feels,
Breathing the air so clean.
But today he runs, not prances,
Terror in his eyes,
As the dogs come after him.
What they were sent for is no lie.
He runs, he runs, he stops.
A gap lies in-between.
He breathes hard, he jumps.
The gap is almost clear,
But then, so suddenly, the gun is raised.
Bang, he drops.
He takes a last, long, agonised look
At the soft, turf-filled hills of green.
There he lies alone, weakened is what he feels.
His happiness is over and done.

Natasha Chapman (10)
Dormers Wells Junior School

THE GHOST

Imagine a ghost,
That came through your post.
You and the ghost were all alone,
Then it started to moan.
What would you do?
I know what I would,
I'd flush him down the loo!

Nasira Patel (10)
Dormers Wells Junior School

DOLPHINS

Dolphins
Swishing through dark blue waves
As dark blue as the night.
A friendly squeak and glint of the eye
Never gives you a fright.
Guess what this dream is.
It's a dolphin.
Our friend arches up through
Laughing and squeaking too.
Clever things - smarty fins
They amuse everyone. They are really fun.
Their skin is as smooth as soap
Dolphins never mope.
Dolphins are the best
Please don't give them a long rest.

Jevanjot Kaur Bhinder (10)
Dormers Wells Junior School

HAPPINESS, SADNESS

Happiness
Happiness sounds like a poem being told,
Happiness feels like touch of gold,
Happiness looks like a boy being healed,
Happiness smells like a delicious meal,
Happiness tastes like a wonderful dinner.

Sadness
Sadness smells like rotten yoghurt,
Sadness feels like dirty mud,
Sadness tastes like disgusting medicine,
Sadness sounds like cries for help.

Mariam Adesanya (10)
Dormers Wells Junior School

WINTER...

Golden leaves died and forgotten.
Bare branches old and alone.
The sharp blade of the chilling wind.
The invisible layer of ice,
The thick coat of white.
A howling wind waiting to come in.

The glistening snowflakes
As they touch the ground.
The raindrops pounding
On the windowpane.

All of the signs something is coming.
Winter is here.
Winter is here.

Saba Awan (10)
Dormers Wells Junior School

TIGERS

Ra, ra, ra, in a cage
Letting out all his rage
All that holds him back are bars
His body a slick, fighting machine
His claws swipe blood clean
His eyes are his own firelight
Watch out or you will die of fright
As powerful as a bear
Just waits for his victim to tear
As for his victim, it's turned to pulp
All it can do is gasp and gulp.

Tharindu Fernando (11)
Dormers Wells Junior School

An Autumn Day

Wind rustling through the trees,
Feel the cold, sharp autumn breeze.
Leaves scattered on the ground,
Footsteps behind don't make a sound.

All animals sound asleep,
Sleeping on the cold, autumn leaves.
Wind howling through the air,
Trees around seem to stare.

Many shades of colours decorate the floor,
Where the fresh, green grass grew before.

Charles Dimitriadis (10)
Dormers Wells Junior School

Who Makes The Dark Scary?

I would watch the floor tonight if I were you,
You don't know what could be there.
I'll give you a clue,
He doesn't have hair.

When the moon shines,
Across the sea of trees,
He scampers along the ground,
But no one ever sees.

He walks along the nearby stream,
Through the window,
Your brother screams.
You rush to his room to see what's wrong
But by then he has gone.

Rebecca Kintoff (10)
Hampton Junior School

IF I WERE A . . .

If I were a unicorn,
I would run through the trees,
Fly to the clouds
With my beautiful wings,
With my white, gleaming coat,
With my smooth, leathery tail,
With my long legs.
I would be stronger than a whale.

Lizzie Foster (10)
Hampton Junior School

WAVES

Splish, splash, I'm the waves
I hurl on the rocks all day
I'm under in the caves
Then out again with a splish, splash
I leave the salty spray on the beach
I'm the waves.

James Birdseye (9)
Hampton Junior School

THERE ONCE WAS A PRINCESS

There once was a princess from Ealing
Who walked upside down on the ceiling
Her knickers fell down
And got caught on her crown
The position was very revealing.

Tom Sheppey, Robert Corr & Sam Imbrey (11)
Hampton Junior School

MY BIG EARS

My big ears,
I hate my big ears,
What use are these big ears?
All I can hear is . . .
A bee buzzing,
A cat purring,
A child sleeping,
A mum shouting,
A dad working,
A baby wailing,
A dog barking,
A car driving,
A person breathing,
A cow mooing,
A bunch of children playing,
A teacher teaching,
An owl hooting,
A spider crawling,
A bird tweeting.
Maybe my big ears are useful after all!

Kiri Poliszewski (8)
Hampton Junior School

A SILENT POEM

It's windy and cold
I can hear the trees swaying
I can smell the pine cones
And the fresh lake
Trickling across the mountain
I can taste the chicken from my tea
And my hot chocolate.

Anaïs Das Gupta (8)
Hampton Junior School

SLEEP

As cold as ice,
As black as the night.
As soft as pure skin,
As loving as lavender.
As I smell the warm fire,
I hear it crackling.
I take a big breath,
Everything comes towards me.
I breathe out,
Everything goes out.
I look around,
Everything is safe.
I go back upstairs,
I have a drink of water.
I lay down on my pillow,
I cannot get to sleep.
I get my cassette player,
I read a book.
I go to sleep.

Evangeline Cundle (8)
Hampton Junior School

THE LOVELY THING I FELT

I had a lovely dream,
Sleeping with my ted.
Until I felt a hand,
Touch my cosy bed.
I liked it so much,
I wanted it even more
And when I woke up,
I saw my mum walk out of the door.

Michael McCubbin (8)
Hampton Junior School

WINGS

If I had wings
I would dance on the moonlight
And soar with the stars.

If I had wings
I would gaze at the planets
In far outer space.

If I had wings
I would venture into the atmosphere
And dance through the sky.

If I had wings
I would dance
To the music of the nightingale.

Sam Harry Kestenbaum (8)
Hampton Junior School

WINGS

If I had wings
I would dance with the snowflakes
On the white of a glossy moonbeam.

If I had wings
I would swoop through all the colours of the rainbow
And feel the gentle touch of a fluffy, white cloud.

If I had wings
I would glide up and over the moon
And wait for it to go down.

Emily Allen (7)
Hampton Junior School

IF I WERE A . . .

If I were a crocodile
I'd swim down the river,
I'd explore the world,
I'd eat and eat till I was full.
I'd gobble up fish
With my big, mighty jaws,
I'd be big and strong
To fight off predators.
I'd watch animals and birds
Up in the sky,
I'd sit sunbathing all day on a rock.

But all that's nonsense,
Well, I can dream
But that's what makes me, me.

Sebastian Jacques (9)
Hampton Junior School

IF I WERE . . .

If I were a dolphin I'd swim from land to land,
I'll visit my friends waiting for me to play,
Swimming over and under looking what's for me.
I go under, what do I see?
I see beautiful scenery,
Magnificent creatures, I'll explore the world.
I see people destroying the coral.
Why would they do that?
I don't know why they would do that.
I do care but what am I to do?
I am just a kid, that's what I am.

Anna Vere-Bujnowski (10)
Hampton Junior School

My Ears And Tongue

I can hear an ant whisper to his mate,
'Look out for that foot. Oh no, there's another one.'
I can hear dust drop on the floor with a thud,
It sounds like a giant walking down a step.
I can hear raindrops scream to the window,
'Mind out of the way.'
I can hear the sun laugh at the moon,
'Not yet.'

I can taste a bun so sweet it feels like I'm in Heaven.
I can taste an apple so sour but sweet.
I can taste a chocolate in my mouth, melting.

Without my ears
And without my tongue
I would not know
What to do.

Sian MacKenzie-Doubleday (9)
Hampton Junior School

I Smell

I smell an ant,
A clock ticking by,
A big, red car speeding along the road,
A big, green plant reaching for the sky.

I smell the sun, the stars,
I smell the planets, the big, glistening moon.

I smell the people up and down the street,
I smell the people in this brilliant world.

Sean Lee Rice (9)
Hampton Junior School

SO SILENT

It was so silent that I heard
Parrots talking
Tigers breathing
Leaves waving
Ants walking on the grass
Snakes slithering in the trees
Creepy-crawlies going up the tree.

It was so silent I could hear
Grasshoppers hopping in the thick, green grass.

It was so peaceful that I felt the tree shake
Because the creepy crawlies were coming up the tree.

It was so calm that I sensed the clouds moving at the top of the tree.

It was so still that I caught the breath of an ant.

Sophie Parslow (8)
Hampton Junior School

SWEETS

I looked through a window and what did I see?

Cola bottles, sugar babies, flying saucers.
I feel the need to buy one!

I got home and ran up to my room and *scoff!*
All in one.

I nearly hit the roof!
It was so sugary I felt all tingly inside.

I thought I would like to do it again some time!

Michael Sheppey (9)
Hampton Junior School

WINGS

If I had wings
I would feel the glossy rainbow shine on me
And twirl through the sun's rays.

If I had wings
I would scoop up the snowflakes
And let them melt away.

If I had wings
I would peek through the gates of Heaven
To watch the angels swoop through the clouds.

If I had wings
I would reach out to touch
The fingertips of the clouds.

Alice Calder (7)
Hampton Junior School

WINGS

If I had wings
I would swoosh through the diamonds sunlight.

If I had wings
I would glide through the slippery snowdrops.

If I had wings
I would be overjoyed to spy the glittering stars.

If I had wings
I would skate through the crackly snowflakes.

George Wilkins (7)
Hampton Junior School

WINGS

If I had wings
I would dance on a rainbow light
And scoop up the colours in my hands.

If I had wings
I would stare at the snowdrops.

If I had wings
I would ride on stars.

If I had wings
I would dance on a rainbow.

If I had wings
I would peep at the birds.

If I had wings
I would stare at the silver moon.

If I had wings
I would sweep under snow
Until the sun shines on me.

Melissa Hampton (7)
Hampton Junior School

WINGS

If I had wings
I would scoop up the silvery raindrops.
I would soar up high to dance on a rainbow.
I could leap up high and land in a fluffy, white cloud.
I would shoot to the moon and have a peep at the other side.

Michael Plumridge (8)
Hampton Junior School

WINGS

If I had wings
I would peek at the birds
That glimmered on the branches of the plant.

If I had wings
I would stare at the glittering silver stars
And dance to the music of the birds.

If I had wings
I would gaze at the patterned butterflies
As they swirled up to the brightness of light.

If I had wings
I would sit on the fluffy clouds
And do my dance to the music of the birds.

If I had wings
I would gaze at the sunshine
And feel the shining fingers of the sun.

If I had wings
I would dance on a rainbow
And scoop up the clouds in my hand.

If I had wings
I would glance at the snowdrops
As they shone in my hand.

If I had wings
I would taste the heat of the shining sun.

Susanna Hall (8)
Hampton Junior School

WINGS

If I had wings
I would gaze at patterned butterflies
As they swirled up to the brightness of light.

If I had wings
I would glide outside into the sunset
And wonder at its beauty.

If I had wings
I would taste the snowdrops on my tongue
As they melted away.

If I had wings
I would bathe in the stars
And seek the rainbow.

If I had wings
I would swoosh
In the crystal clear raindrops.

Harriet Fraser (7)
Hampton Junior School

WINGS

If I had wings
I would dance with the stars in the dusky moonlight.

If I had wings
I would twirl and twist with the sparkling butterflies.

If I had wings
I would ride on a snowflake as it swirled to the ground.

Matty Humphrey (7)
Hampton Junior School

IF I WERE . . .

If I were a bird I would tweet sweetly in the morning
And then set off to explore another city.

I would eat worms and insects
And be happy being a bird.

I could glide through the sky every day
And see all sorts of new things every day
And it would look beautiful.

I would swoop down from the sky
And drink water and peck at the food on the ground.

I wouldn't wear anything.
I would wear clothes and wear shoes
But not wear socks.

Daniel Gale (10)
Hampton Junior School

WINGS

If I had wings
I would glide with the jewelled butterflies.

If I had wings
I would swirl in the sky with the clouds and the birds.

If I had wings
I would peep through the rainbow and put the colours in my pocket.

If I had wings
I would taste the snowflakes and let them melt away in my hands.

Charlotte Firth (7)
Hampton Junior School

If I Were . . .

If I were a shooting star,
I would make wishes come true,
I'd swoosh through the night,
With my sparks shining bright,
My gold, shining body,
My silvery, glistening smile,
Will put you to sleep,
In just a little while.

If I were a shooting star,
I would be awake all night,
In my velvety, black sky,
Watching, wondering, waiting
To cast my spells on you,
So watch for my magic light,
As I glide past your window with delight,
Look for my smile because I'll be looking for yours.

I'm only dreaming but I wish that it could be true!

Kayleigh Bower (9)
Hampton Junior School

Wings

If I had wings
I would swim in fluffy clouds.

If I had wings
I would visit Father Christmas every day.

If I had wings
I would pounce from star to star with planets to gaze at.

Alexander Morris (7)
Hampton Junior School

WINGS

If I had wings
I would skate to the moon
And have a piece of cheese.

If I had wings
I would glide through the clouds
And have a little sleep.

If I had wings
I would float past the stars
And then I would fly past the sun and moon.

If I had wings
I would zoom to the shop for my mummy
And buy some dinner or our tea.

If I had wings
I would shoot to my nanny's
And see if they are okay.

Emily Cheshire (8)
Hampton Junior School

THE SCARY DREAM

I was having a scary dream
I was in an invisible room
Some people were trying to get me
I thought they were going to get me
They were going to kill me . . .
Until someone woke me up!

Ahad Noor (8)
Hampton Junior School

ICE CREAM

Ice cream, ice cream
It's most people's dream
A ninety-nine with extra cream

Cheeky, chocolate chip
Don't let it drip

Soft strawberry sundae
You can even eat it on Monday

Fabulous five-inch flake
It's more like a cake

Nifty ninety-nine
Always a good sign

Suave, sophisticated, strawberry sauce
It's my favourite topping, of course!

Joseph Allen (10)
Hampton Junior School

WHAT MY BIG EARS CAN HEAR?

I can hear
The wind making the trees sway
And an aeroplane crashing into a cloud.
I can hear my cat in the grass.
I can hear people breathing in their sleep.
Taps dripping, people going for a walk.
That's what I can hear.

Georgina Rhoades-Brown (8)
Hampton Junior School

LISTEN

It was so quiet
You could hear
Trees groaning
About the wind.
It was so quiet
You could hear
Plants reaching
To get the best sun.
I was so quiet
You could hear
The rain making
A whoosh noise
As it falls down.
It was so quiet
You could hear
Everything tingle
In your ear.

Katie Bulford (8)
Hampton Junior School

IN THE JUNGLE

It was so silent in the jungle
That I heard
Trees swaying
Birds singing
Footprints in the mud
That you can hear
Leaves on the ground
Rain on the trees dropping down.

Adam Bartlett (9)
Hampton Junior School

So Silent

It was so silent
That I heard
Squirrels putting nuts
In the bark of trees
And planning where they are.

It was so tranquil
That I heard
A caterpillar slithering
Across the grass.

It was so peaceful
That I heard
Bats swooping
Around the cave.

Thomas Coggins (8)
Hampton Junior School

Water

Water in your taps,
Water in your hose,
Water in your sink,
Water in your bath,
Water in your shower,
Water in your toilet,
Water in the pond,
Water in the river,
Water in the sea,
Water in the ocean,
Water everywhere.

Daniel Hollands (9)
Hampton Junior School

It Was So Silent That I Heard . . .

It was so silent that I heard the teddy stitching up his torn leg,
It was so windless that I listened to the soldier mumbling while trying
to find his hat.
It was so noiseless, but the best busy day filled my head
And suddenly the constant chattering of the dolls broke the silence.
It was so hushed that I started again to wonder about the next day
But this time it wasn't the dolls that broke the silence
It was the bright morning horizon.

Emily Lavagna (8)
Hampton Junior School

I Can Hear

I can hear the heaven's rain tingling like a crystal,
I can hear the hell's bang, banging like a pistol.

I can hear the winter coming ever closer and closer,
I can hear the sun complaining rays like a toaster.

I can hear the sparks spitting to each other,
I can hear the plastic screaming for cover.

Melissa Paris (8)
Hampton Junior School

So Silent

It was so silent that I heard someone putting warm towels on top of me.
It was so gentle that I sensed the airing cupboard door closing quietly.
It was so peaceful that I felt the warm float around me.
It was so quiet that I listened to the light in the room go out.
Everything was calm and still.

Sarah Carter (8)
Hampton Junior School

WINGS

If I had wings
I would dance to the music of the nightingale

If I had wings
I would swoosh over the highest mountain
And soar over their shining vanilla snowcaps

If I had wings
I would gaze at the winter robin's colours

If I had wings
I would slide over the slippery moon
And seek the dusky moonlight

If I had wings
I would taste the sun's rays as hot as Mexican chilli.

Adam Amhama (8)
Hampton Junior School

IF I WERE . . .

If I were Hasselbaink I would score over 200 goals for Chelsea,
I would wear the no 9 shirt.
It's blue and it's got a bit of white on it.
My team leader, Gudjohnsen, would keep on setting me up.
I'd score every goal if I could and I'd be in the World Book of
Records for my excellent club Chelsea!
I would have an exotic house covered in gold bricks.
My holidays would be great, spent in paradise
Enjoying eating fabulous food is great
From pizza to pasta, chipolatas to tarts.
I would love to be him!

Benjamin Pain (10)
Hampton Junior School

IF I WERE ...

If I were a parrot I would let the wind carry me
Watching the scenery go by.
The exotic plants and the shine on the trees.
I'd fly over waterfalls that gleam.

I'd go on adventures to see the world.
Yes.
The pyramids of Egypt,
The rivers of many lands,
Mountains in Nepal,
The rainforests of Brazil.

This bird I can't be
But it's fine being me.

James Morris (10)
Hampton Junior School

THE BIG VOLCANO

It was so silent that I heard
Lava under my feet
Like tea falling on a hand.

It was so quiet that I listened
To bubbles popping in the lava
In a constant beat.

It was so peaceful that I heard
Rocks falling into the volcano
In little heaps.

It was so calm that I listened
To rock cracking at the sight.

Cara Smith (8)
Hampton Junior School

UNDERGROUND

It was so silent
That I heard . . .
The worms slither
Through the mud
And snails going past
With big shells on their backs.

It was so calm
That I heard
A centipede's leg
Get caught on a twig.

It was so peaceful
That I heard
The doves flying by,
Their soft wings were white.

Harmanpreet Kaur (8)
Hampton Junior School

CHOCOLATE

C   hocolate is heavenly.
H   azelnuts in chocolate spoil the taste.
O   h, if I had chocolate all day.
C   adbury's, Mars, Nestlé!
O   h, I'd give anything to taste some sweet,
L   uxurious caramel bars.
A   dream so far away.
T   he chocolate is drifting away, I
E   njoy chocolate when I have the chance!

Caitlin Bartholomew (9)
Hampton Junior School

MY DREAM

Flying, not dying
No one is crying
Unicorns, giants
Not like science
Fairytale creatures
Lots more features

No war, no gore
No one is poor
Everyone gets along
The birds sing a song
Joy and happiness in the air
Everyone says a little prayer

The dolphins are swimming
Bells are ringing
People are enjoying themselves
Reading books off golden shelves

Magic around, magic about
Teapots talk through their spout
Fun and joy
Is a nice little toy
No one minds
Being nice and kind
And that's my imaginative dream.

Joseph P Courtley (10)
Hampton Junior School

IT WAS SO SILENT THAT I HEARD

It was so silent that I heard
Ants eating and caterpillars crunching.
It was so calm that I could hear
The wind swishing through the tops of the green trees.

It was so gentle that I felt
A little, fluffy spider crawling up my arm.
It was so quiet I could hear
Birds singing a sweet song.

Ella Harding (9)
Hampton Junior School

I WOULD LIKE TO BE . . .

I would like to be a sailor sailing out to sea
With my cat and me.
I could find buried treasure
And be rich forever.
I could be a good storyteller for children
On my adventure.

I would like to be a fireman
Rescuing people from burning buildings,
Getting a lot of lives that were in a lot of danger
Or being behind the big hose
And putting out a roaring fire.

I would like to be a tennis player
Who won cups that shone like superstars
And fans that cheer like people at a theatre
But they should be watching me
Like they ought to be.

I would like to be an athlete winning races
Getting more gold medals than Steven Redgrave
Being more famous than David Beckham
And being the fastest in the world
But I am what I am
But I can dream.

Dominic Paul Futter (10)
Hampton Junior School

IMAGINATIONS

Flying to stars, driving cars
Singing and playing guitars
Going to space, winning a race
Being famous must be ace

Swimming and skating
Dancing and diving
Artists and sculptors
Designers and writers

Comedy, horror, thrillers and more
Hook, The Lion King and James Bond
Famous people act in these
I wonder if I ever could?

Imaginations, imaginations
I wish they could be true
Being on the Titanic
But one of the surviving crew.

Nathan Blyth (10)
Hampton Junior School

THE OLD DOG

It was so silent that I heard . . .
The dog's heart pant
At a fast speed
And the dog's muscles
Moan with pain
And the bones
Grind together like a knife cutting bread
And the old dog lying at the cold, dark depth of the moon
And the body resting for another day's hard work.

Thomas Headford (9)
Hampton Junior School

WINGS

If I had wings
I would zoom through the clouds
And shoot down on Earth.

If I had wings
I would bounce up and down
Then I would glide past Mars.

If I had wings
I would sleep on the clouds
Then I would float like a bird.

If I had wings
I would jump like a bunny rabbit
In the sky.

If I had wings
I would shoot like a bullet
And I would zoom into the sky.

Shane Nolan (8)
Hampton Junior School

I WISH I WAS FAMOUS

I wish I was famous like Britney Spears,
I wish I was famous throughout the years.
I wish I was famous like Roald Dahl,
I wish I was famous in the record file.
I wish I was famous like the Queen,
I wish I was famous, clever and keen.
I wish I was famous like people on TV,
I wish I was famous, that's for me!

Mark Winterburn (10)
Hampton Junior School

A Lion In The Jungle

A lion in the jungle
Makes some sound,
He hits his paw
Upon the ground.

Lion in the jungle
Go away,
Poor old lion
He has been gone all day.

Lion in the jungle
Come back here,
I feel safe
When you are near.

Lion in the jungle
Don't be shy,
Come out and see
The beautiful sky.

Lion in the jungle
I'm your friend,
This friendship
Will never end.

Tyler Shelmerdine (9)
Hampton Junior School

Swan

It is like an angel
Flowing down the stream
As white as the dove.

Sally Gardner (10)
Hampton Junior School

I CAN HEAR . . .

I can hear a bumblebee
As loud as a ticking clock.
I can hear an oval egg
Cracking on the top.
I can hear the smallest thing
You could ever know.
I can hear elephants and bears
Like a herd, very slow!

Annabel Bartlett (9)
Hampton Junior School

IF I WERE . . .

If I were king I would
Give £10,000 to the poor,
Rule the country and be good,
Be lively,
Eat sweets
And I'd be funny and play.

Raman Jerome (9)
Hampton Junior School

RIVERS

Silvery and flowing
Gentle and rough
Always moving, never stops.

Kelly Hardy (11)
Hampton Junior School

SWISHING, SWAYING STREAMS

Swishing, swaying streams
Go through the rapid rain.

Gurgling, guzzling gutters
Go round the water drain.

Luscious, leaky lake finds the rushing rain
Around the water and down the drain.

Rivers flowing, rivers flowing, flowing
Like a twister.

Waves racing, waves racing, racing
Like a raindrop.

Swishing, swaying streams
Swishing, swaying streams.

Lucie Sarah Cassius (10)
Hampton Junior School

TROPICAL FISH

I am a tropical fish
Who lives in the sea.
Why don't you have
A look at me?
I dive down deep
I look quite neat
The other fishes
Envy me!

Jonathan Bestley (9)
Hampton Junior School

ZEBRA

Zebra, zebra
Black and white
Watch out
It will give you
A fright.
On the plains
It runs
And plays
Little zebra
Happy days.
Under
The sunset
It drinks
From the stream
Black and white
It looks
Supreme.
Its beady eyes look at me.
I wonder what it may see?
Its stripes are black, its body white.
My little zebra in the moonlight.

Hannah Mabb (10)
Hampton Junior School

RIVERS

Bishing, bashing, blue seas
Full of frisky fish gliding easily
Through the water with the whales and sharks.
Bothersome beetles lounging in a lovely lake
Hoping they won't get eaten by a hungry drake.

Steven Hall (10)
Hampton Junior School

ANIMALS

Dolphins dive in the sea,
Monkeys leap from tree to tree.
Owls search for food in the night,
A robin sings in the morning light.
Lions lie in the sun
While the cubs decide to have some fun.
There's a snake, what a fright,
I wonder if it bites?
Polar bears play in the ice
While domestic cats go hunting for mice.
An elephant flaps its ears,
How amazing, it's been around for years.

Victoria Brice (10)
Hampton Junior School

A GOLDFISH!

As cold as ice,
As dark as night,
As scaly as a dragon,
As blunt as a pencil.
I'm a fish!
As warm as fire,
As shiny as silver,
As special as money,
As flat as a brick.
I am gold!

I'm a goldfish!

Hannah Manzur (8)
Hampton Junior School

WINGS

If I had wings
    I would jump as high as the sky
        And swim through the air

If I had wings
    I would dive into pools of clouds

If I had wings
    I would float to the moon
        And shoot back down again

If I had wings
    I would whizz around the world
        And zoom back the other way.

Alice Simmons (8)
Hampton Junior School

WINGS

If I had wings
    I would swim through
        The clouds.

If I had wings
    I would jump as high as the sky
        And swim through the air.

If I had wings
    I would dive
        To the sea.

Jessica Kravetz (8)
Hampton Junior School

RAPID RIVER

Rapid river running right,
Wriggling throughout the starry night.

Rapid river running round and round,
Making a swishing and swaying sound.

Rapid river rushing down a rumbling bend,
Rippling round rocks at its frothy end.

Rapid river racing up and down,
Running free throughout the town.

Rapid river, rippling through the brook,
Twisting and turning to get a better look.

Oliver Fallows (9)
Hampton Junior School

THE HUNTER

As the leaping lion approaches,
Anticipation waits all around.
Grazing zebras, staggering stags,
Expect the prance, pounce and leap.

The great growl, scowl and roar,
Echo like thunder through Africa.
Hungry hunters are giants towering,
The lioness lies under her shady tree.

Worn out wildebeest wonder when . . .
The fierce roar will approach again.
Tired they lie down to rest.

Sophie Fountain (10)
Hampton Junior School

PILES OF PERFECT PASTA

Piles of perfect pasta,
Twisty twirls and creamy curls
Two piles of perfect pasta
Chewy tubes and saucy shells
Four piles of perfect pasta

Marvellous macaroni and fabulous farfalle
Add it all up to make six piles of perfect pasta
I have got slurpy spaghetti tonight
Twist it, twirl it round the fork
Then stuff it in my mouth

Oops, some landed on my lap
Quick, brush it off before Mum comes!

Ellen Sellwood (10)
Hampton Junior School

ICE

Ice, ice, freezing cold,
Icicles, new or old,
Put it in the sun and it will melt,
Turn to rain and start to pelt.

Frozen ice, in a rapid river,
Frozen ice, in a water reservoir,
Frozen ice, in the fridge,
Freezing into the blocks
That you have in your drink.

Ben Allen (10)
Hampton Junior School

A World Of Wonder Reached By Me

Far, far away
Over the valley
Over the sea
Over the ocean
There's a beautiful land
For me
For me
Just for me.

The air is so cold it boils my blood
The lilies are so sweet I'm in a daze
The moon is as bright as the sun
All the same I'll brave the valley tonight
The air is bitter but that won't stop me
The sea is roaring
The wind is howling but that won't stop me
I've jumped in the rowing boat and set sail for the land of beauty.

I'm almost there, land's in sight
The fairies are singing so sweetly I could sleep
Even the puppies are sweet here.
Suddenly there's a sound, a soft noise
It gushes so sweetly, it's Mum calling me
So I'll set sail again and go home to my mum
There she is, her arms open wide
She's as soft as silk, no, she's softer than silk.

Hannah Lunniss (9)
Hampton Junior School

Sights

I can see my hands, covered with loads of germs.
I can see spaghetti, wriggling around like worms.
I can see the sun shining very bright.
I can see a daffodil, what a pretty sight.

I can see a raindrop falling from the sky.
I can see a bird flying very high.
I can see the moon twinkling in the night.
I can see a fox run away with fright.

Emily Deadman (9)
Hampton Junior School

WINGS

If I had wings
    I would glide to the moon
        And take some cheese down to Earth.

If I had wings
    I would *zooooom* round the world
        And race the stars.

If I had wings
    I would fly and get a moon rock
        And take it down to Earth.

If I had wings
    I would sleep in the clouds
        And run on the moon.

If I had wings
    I would fly in and out of the stars.

If I had wings
    I would fly down to my football club and Beavers.

If I had wings
    I would race the shooting stars.

Jake Calver (7)
Hampton Junior School

I'd Rather Be Me!

I'd rather be me
Than a bumblebee,
You can do more things
And no more stings!

You can run in the garden and play with your friends
Only if the weather's nice, it all depends.

I'd rather be me
Than my Uncle Ben,
He only speaks to me now and then.
He's always watching the TV
Instead of playing games with me.

I'd rather be me
Than a little, brown mouse,
I couldn't live in a tiny house
Or under the floorboard,
Scurry around
Making a meal
From what I've found.

There's a nice crumb
In that floppy, old hat
Oh my word
Here comes the . . .

Cat!

Emmie Collis (10)
Hampton Junior School

Banquets

Banquets buzzing, belly buttons bursting
Feasting on fine food, feeling full.
Colourful clothes, dazzling decorations
Dancing through the night.

Clicking, clashing, *cheers*
Go the partying people
Who are having
Fantastic fireworking fun.

David Simmons (9)
Hampton Junior School

RABBITS

Rabbits white, big and small;
Wriggly rabbits nibbling grass.
Rabbits, rabbits climbing tall;
Twitchy tails as they pass.
Rabbits white, big and small.

I wish I had a rabbit as a pet;
I'd call it Nosy Nibbly Nickles.
Put up a sign saying 'Rabbits To Let';
My sister and I would feed it pickles.
I wish I had a rabbit as a pet.

All rabbits nice, big and fluffy;
Or scruffy, little, hairy heads.
I like the small one all very puffy;
My sister likes Mr Fidgety Fred.
All rabbits nice, big and fluffy.

Come on, readers, get a rabbit;
Everyone's got one so why don't you get one too?
It's got to become one of your habits;
Why don't you play with it peek a boo?
Come on, readers, get a rabbit.

Yvonne Yue-Fong Chan (9)
Hampton Junior School

WINGS

If I had wings
    I would skate on the wind's light, smooth breath
        And touch the sweet candyfloss clouds.

If I had wings
    I would taste a chunk out of the fiery, meatball sun.

If I had wings
    I would stroke the soft, poodle skin
        Of the clouds.

If I had wings
    I would catch the snowdrops
        And watch them melt into my hands.

If I had wings
    I would gaze at the sunset going down
        And the fiery reds bursting out of it.

If I had wings
    I would dream of gliding softly to different planets
        And meeting different kinds of creatures.

Elinor Bolsh (8)
Hampton Junior School

WINGS

If I had wings
    I would sleep on the soft clouds
        And dream of lovely things.

If I had wings
    I would zoom through the stars
        And touch everyone when I went by.

If I had wings
   I would jump up
      And the breeze would take me to a planet.

If I had wings
   I would swim through the clouds
      And glide into the breeze.

Alice Farrar (8)
Hampton Junior School

WINGS

If I had wings
   I would glide straight through the clouds
      And float into the stars.

If I had wings
   I would float to the moon
      And glide to the sun.

If I had wings
   I would shoot to the moon
      And take a piece of cheese.

If I had wings
   I would float to the sky
      And sing with the birds.

If I had wings
   I would dance on the clouds
      And leap to the sky.

Lauren Bartholomew (8)
Hampton Junior School

WINGS

If I had wings
    I would touch the sweet candyfloss cloud
        And skate on the wind's smooth breath.

If I had wings
    I would grab the shiny ball of gold sun
        And swing the ball of gold whilst I am floating.

If I had wings
    I would stroke Father Christmas's fluffy, beardy cloud
        When I fly to the North Pole.

If I had wings
    I would slide down the rainbow
        And shout, 'Yippee!'

If I had wings
    I would gaze at the people
        Who look like little ants running around.

If I had wings
    I would dance on the tops of the trees
        And walk on the rooftops.

Rachel Brooker (8)
Hampton Junior School

WINGS

If I had wings
    I would swing in my imagination
        And swim in the nice, cool air.

If I had wings
    I would whizz round and round
        And get really whizzy and dizzy.

If I had wings
    I would spin like a spinning top
        And lay in a cloud afterwards.

If I had wings
    I would dance in the sky
        And sing a lullaby.

Jamie Smith (8)
Hampton Junior School

WINGS

If I had wings
    I would shoot to the sky
        And glide over the clouds.

If I had wings
    I would race the angels
        And try and race as fast as I could.

If I had wings
    I would float to the moon
        And take some cheese.

If I had wings
    I would fly across the world
        And touch the moon.

If I had wings
    I would touch the sky
        And float in space.

Jack Curant (7)
Hampton Junior School

WINGS

If I had wings
 I would eat the sweet, fluffy candyfloss clouds
  And dance on the wind's breath.

If I had wings
 I would fly to the sun
  And peel it like a juicy, ripe orange.

If I had wings
 I would jump and jump and jump
  On the fluffy clouds.

If I had wings
 I would slide down
  A rainbow.

If I had wings
 I would stare and stare
  At the Great Wall of China.

If I had wings
 I would dream of,
  I would climb on too,
   The top of the trees
    And jump on the clouds, step by step.

Giulia Davidson (7)
Hampton Junior School

WINGS

If I had wings
 I would skid on the clouds
  And glide through stars.

If I had wings
 I would zoom across the top of the sea
  And float on the breath of the wind.

If I had wings
I would eat chunks of the sun
To keep me flying.

If I had wings
I would fly on the cold ice
I would zoom through the sun
And step on the cotton wool clouds.

Andrew Park (7)
Hampton Junior School

WINGS

If I had wings
I would eat candyfloss
From the cloud.

If I had wings
I would eat a slice of cheese
From the moon.

If I had wings
I would glide
To the planet Mars.

If I had wings
I would zoom
Straight past the moon.

If I had wings
I would see all the planets
In space.

Katie Downes (7)
Hampton Junior School

WINGS

If I had wings
  I would touch the sweet, fluffy, candyfloss clouds
    And skate on the wind's smooth breath.

If I had wings
  I would glide to the sunlight
    And peel it like a ripe orange.

If I had wings
  I would eat the head of a snowman!

If I had wings
  I would slide down a rainbow.

If I had wings
  I would gaze at all the people
    Like little ants.

If I had wings
  I would dream of eating the sand
    And walk on the fruit.

Billie Elgar (7)
Hampton Junior School

WINGS

If I had wings
  I would glide in the air
    And shout so loud

If I had wings
  I would swim in the air
    And jump in the clouds

If I had wings
    I would do a backflip
        And show off to my friends

If I had wings
    I would zoom through the air
        And glide on the air.

Shiv Jalota (8)
Hampton Junior School

WINGS

If I had wings
    I would touch the sweet, candyfloss clouds
        And skate on the wind's breath.

If I had wings
    I would float and dodge the sun
        Like a dragon's fireball.

If I had wings
    I would hop from cloud to cloud.

If I had wings
    I would ride a tornado.

If I had wings
    I would stare at the Great Wall of China.

If I had wings
    I would dream of serving volcano
        And climbing the seas.

Jay Newton (8)
Hampton Junior School

WINGS

If I had wings
I would touch the moon
And eat all the cheese.

If I had wings
I would *zoooooom* through the clouds
And get soaked.

If I had wings
I would sleep on the clouds
And see my friend's house.

If I had wings
I would eat the sun
As hot as fire.

If I had wings
I would do some back flips
And show-off to my friends.

If I had wings
I would glide off a leaf
And touch the clouds.

If I had wings
I would get a star
And give it to you!

If I had wings
I would go to Mars
And bring chocolate for you.

Patch Smith (7)
Hampton Junior School

ME AND MY WINGS

If I had wings
    I would walk on water and feel it on my feet

If I had wings
    I would do back flips
        And show-off to my friends Jake and Shiv

If I had wings
    I would swim through the sky
        Like swimming in the sea or a pool

If I had wings
    I would zoom through the sky
        Like a racing car or a bus and a lorry

If I had wings
    I would touch the clouds
        And take some down to Earth

If I had wings
    I would glide in the air
        Like a bird

If I had wings
    I would race the wind
        And it would push me to fly faster
        And faster

If I had wings
    I would fly up to the moon
        And touch it.

Callum Cronin (8)
Hampton Junior School

WINGS

If I had wings
    I would zoom to the shop

If I had wings
    I would bounce to the trees

If I had wings
    I would sleep in the sky

If I had wings
    I would run in the clouds

If I had wings
    I would skip to the moon

If I had wings
    I would fly to the stars

If I had wings
    I would jump to school.

Sophie Thompson (8)
Hampton Junior School

MY CAT

My sneaky, silky, silly cat,
Is as white as winter.
My miaowing, mental cat is mad.
My fat, friendly cat likes Felix for his dinner.
My gentle, generous cat
Gave me green glass.
My perfect, playful pet is wonderful.

Zoe Alexander (9)
Hampton Junior School

WINGS

If I had wings
  I would taste the sugary,
    Sweet, candy clouds.

If I had wings
  I would glide to the sun
    And peel it like an orange.

If I had wings
  I would slide down a rainbow
    And ride the squealing dolphins.

If I had wings
  I would stare at the tiny ants
    That crawled on the Earth.

If I had wings
  I would look for the treasure
    Under the swaying sea.

Alice Courtley (7)
Hampton Junior School

THE MAN FROM DEVON

There was a man from Devon,
Who lived to seventy-seven,
  Along came a bus,
  Without any fuss,
Sent him straight up to Heaven.

James McSweeney & Robert Fennell (11)
Hampton Junior School

WINGS

If I had wings
    I would shoot up to the moon
        And eat all the moon.

If I had wings
    I would sleep
        On the soft, cool clouds.

If I had wings
    I would glide into the water
        Like a bird.

If I had wings
    I would zoom and bounce tree to tree
        And fly to France from England.

Emily Cassius (7)
Hampton Junior School

WINGS

If I had wings
I would swoop through the bright blue sky.

If I had wings
I would doze in the blankety clouds all day.

If I had wings
I would peek through the starlight
And watch for doves passing by.

If I had wings
I would climb into my soft, snuggly, cloud bed.

Trudy Bryan-Kerr (8)
Hampton Junior School

WINGS

If I had wings
    I would count the stars
        On the moon.

If I had wings
    I would eat a slice of cheese
        From the moon.

If I had wings
    I would glide
        Through the air.

If I had wings
    I would swim through the clouds
        And glide into the breeze.

Paige Sturton-Newman (7)
Hampton Junior School

WINGS

If I had wings
I would swirl with the butterflies

If I had wings
I would flutter through the breeze

If I had wings
I would swim with the stars

If I had wings
I would leap with the snowdrops

If I had wings
I would fiddle with the glittery clouds.

Ellie Deakin (8)
Hampton Junior School

WINGS

If I had wings
    I would skate to the moon
        And have a piece of cheese.

If I had wings
    I would rest on the clouds.

If I had wings
    I would wave to my friends.

If I had wings
    I would glide straight through the clouds.

If I had wings
    I would skid on the clouds.

If I had wings
    I would taste the candyfloss from the clouds.

Amber Johnston (7)
Hampton Junior School

WINGS

If I had wings
I would swoop through the snowy ice in a winter age.

If I had wings
I would sneak through the pink, puffy clouds.

If I had wings
I would leap through the pink glow of sunrise.

If I had wings
I would soar through the moonlight and stars
Hanging in the sky's black curtain.

James Caley (8)
Hampton Junior School

WINGS

If I had wings
I would scoop up the warm, yellow sunray.

If I had wings
I would skip through the silvery raindrops.

If I had wings
I would soar through the colourful rainbow.

If I had wings
I would glide like an aeroplane through the glittery clouds.

If I had wings
I would swoosh up to the starlight
And then shoot down to the glittery moonlight.

Scott Thompson (7)
Hampton Junior School

MAGIC

If I had wings
I would swim in the multicoloured rainbow spray

If I had wings
I would scoop up the cold, vanilla ice cream moon's crust

If I had wings
I would skip through the crisp clouds and the spiky stars

If I had wings
I would gaze at birds and bees in the sunlight

If I had wings
I would swoop under the crispy snowdrops and snowflakes
                                                    until the sun set.

Myles Humphrey (8)
Hampton Junior School

MY WONDERFUL LAND

My wonderful land is full with lovely, luscious stuff,
Chocolate houses, sherbet flowers,
You enter a dark, marble door,
And you are somewhere totally different,
Someone eats an apple
And has mystical, magical powers,
In my wonderful, luscious, lovely land.

In my wonderful, luscious, lovely land,
If you imagine something that's there,
In a powerful puff,
Because my wonderful land is full
With lovely, luscious stuff.

You are never angry,
You are always glad,
You are never grumpy,
And certainly never sad.

In my wonderful, luscious, lovely land,
Then suddenly there is a piercing scream,
It goes, 'Natalie, get up!' in a growly way.
I realise my wonderful, luscious land
Is my boring bed.
My mystical dream is over!
In my lovely, luscious land.

Natalie Sen (10)
Hampton Junior School

THE EAGLE

Soaring silently through the air
Flying feathers, fluttering everywhere
Beaks beckoning, bellowing loud.
Can you find it in the clouds?

Eagle eggs like precious jewels
Claws clutch carefully just like tools
Danger dawning, don't look back
Eagle's coming to attack.

Jordon Foskett (10)
Hampton Junior School

ALL DAY LONG

The beach is fun when I'm in the sun
All day long.
The seaside is fun when I'm in the waves
Splashing and thrashing
All day long.
Jumping and diving into the sea
As whales and dolphins swim with me
All day long . . .

Then I'm suddenly afraid -
Out of the water I wade
And stand safe on the beach
Where no shark can reach . . .

In the sand with a spade
I build castles, dismayed
For I came here to be
All day in the sea.

As the sun yawns and lowers his head
Both the day and I are ready for bed . . .
I know that tomorrow I'll return
So I'll not fret -
For I'll swim *all day long*
Before the sun sets . . .

Chelsea Ramsay (9)
Hampton Junior School

My Ears And Eyes

I can hear something, let's see,
It's a buzzing bumblebee.
It whizzes around
But never drops to the ground.

I can hear something again,
It sounds like Big Ben.
Oh no, it's not, it's my grandfather clock.
It's as loud as a drum
And it's my favourite one.

I can see
My apple tree
With his arms outstretched
Beckoning to me.

I can see
My cat Susie
Seeking attention from my little sister Josie.

Without my ears and without my eyes
I'd never be able to be truly alive.

Alexandra Chamberlain (9)
Hampton Junior School

If I Were A . . .

If I were a princess
I would wear long dresses,
Have big feasts and share my food.
I would send my army to fight other countries,
I would order my guards to threaten people
Who stood outside my gates and groaned.

I would scare away witches
Who lived in faraway lands
Until a gleaming white horse appeared in the distance
Carrying a handsome prince
Ready to take me away.

Bryony Curtis (9)
Hampton Junior School

BUMBLEBEE

Bumblebee,
Buzzing busily.
Orange and black,
Sting attack.

Bumblebee,
Bumblebee.

Curious, quick-witted queen,
Making sure she sees a perfect scene.
Hive full of glistening, golden honey.

Bumblebee,
Bumblebee.

Thousands, hundreds, maybe more,
Making honey, running, pours.
Work together, signal, sign,
Make sure everything's fine.

Bumblebee,
Bumblebee.

Hanging hive up a tree,
Until the tree is cut and chopped,
And the hive dies and drops.

Lucy Godwin (10)
Hampton Junior School

WINGS

If I had wings
    I would touch the sweet, candyfloss clouds
        And slide on the wind's smooth breath

If I had wings
    I would glide up to the sun and drink it
        Like an overflowing glass of oranges

If I had wings
    I would float up to the cloud
        And then all the feathers would fall on top of me

If I had wings
    I would fly up and slide down the rainbow
        And find the pot of gold

If I had wings
    I would watch the Monopoly board world
        And its controllers

If I had wings
    I would dream that I was dancing
        On rooftops.

Robert Gilroy (7)
Hampton Junior School

WINGS

If I had wings
I would peek down through the blankety clouds
At the people scurrying about like ants.

If I had wings
I would swim in the sunset whilst watching the shy, melting
Snowflakes fluttering to the cold grass of a child's garden.

If I had wings
I would stroke the glittering sunlight
And twirl with the angels.

If I had wings
I would dance around
Listening to the wonderful song of the nightingale.

Claire Park (7)
Hampton Junior School

WINGS

If I had wings
    I would like the sweet, pink, candyfloss clouds
        And skate on the wind's cold breath.

If I had wings
    I would peel off sweet orange skin
        Off the sun.

If I had wings
    I would stroke the fluffy poodles
        In the light blue sky.

If I had wings
    I would catch the raindrops
        That fall from the sky.

If I had wings
    I would watch the tiny dots
        Working on Earth.

If I had wings
    I would dream of work on the ceiling
        And the light will be on the floor.

Gemma Brien (8)
Hampton Junior School

WINGS

If I had wings
    I would touch the sweet, fluffy, candyfloss cloud
        And skate on the wind's smooth breath.

If I had wings
    I would float and dodge the sun
        Like a dragon's fireball.

If I had wings
    I would throw snowballs at aeroplanes
        And they are so soft that when they touch the roof
                        they evaporate!

If I had wings
    I would fly up and down
        Like watching some thunder flashing up and down.

If I had wings
    I would gaze at the Great Wall of China like a statue.

If I had wings
    I would ride on any rainbow
        And look for treasure at the end.

Richard John Park (7)
Hampton Junior School

WINGS

If I had wings
I would glide in the moonlight with the fluffy clouds.

If I had wings
I would fly into a wall of falling snowflakes.

If I had wings
I would swoop through the stardust shining in the night sky.

If I had wings
I would make a snowman out of the snow-sprinkled clouds.

Myles Wheeler (7)
Hampton Junior School

WINGS

If I had wings
  I would taste the sweet, fluffy, candyfloss clouds
    And breathe the wind's smooth breath

If I had wings
  I would glide to the sun
    And peel it like a ripe, juicy orange

If I had wings
  I would taste the lovely snowballs
    That fall from the sky

If I had wings
  I would slide down the rainbow
    And listen to the raindrops

If I had wings
  I would watch the tiny dots move around
    And watch the ants walk about

If I had wings
  I would climb up trees
    And slide on the rooftops.

Sian F Jolley (7)
Hampton Junior School

WINGS

If I had wings
  I would touch the sweet, fluffy, candyfloss clouds
    And skate on the wind's smooth breath.

If I had wings
  I would glide to the sun and peel it
    Like a juicy, ripe orange then bite a bit off it.

If I had wings
  I would stroke the cold, ice snowman
    And see if it talks.

If I had wings
  I would taste a drop of the rain
    And see if it tastes the same.

If I had wings
  I would look at the tiny ants
    Go in the little Monopoly board's house.

If I had wings
  I would dream of sliding on a rainbow
    And go looking for treasure.

Jamie Thomas Sones (7)
Hampton Junior School

WINGS

If I had wings
I would fly up to the stars.

If I had wings
I would fly through the stormy clouds
Until I found the starlight.

If I had wings
I would call to the rainbow until sunset.

If I had wings
I would dance with the stars until the morning.

Katie Wilson (7)
Hampton Junior School

WINGS

If I had wings
    I would touch the sweet, fluffy, candyfloss clouds
        And dance on the wind's smooth breath.

If I had wings
    I would stop a fiery meatball from hitting the Earth
        And be the hero.

If I had wings
    I would throw snowballs down to the Earth
        And get hit back.

If I had wings
    I would ride a tornado till I was dizzy
        And fall over.

If I had wings
    I would stare at the Great Wall of China
        Like a statue.

If I had wings
    I would dance on the trees
        And walk on rooftops like Father Christmas.

Kyle Fegan (8)
Hampton Junior School

WINGS

If I had wings
I would dance with the starlight and breathe in the air

If I had wings
I would doze in the blankety clouds

If I had wings
I would swoop over the moonlight

If I had wings
I would peek through the clouds to see if someone was hiding there

If I had wings
I would glide through the glittering, shining starlight

If I had wings
I would listen to the raindrops chatter on their way to the ground.

Charlie Bartlett (7)
Hampton Junior School

WINGS

If I had wings
I would swoop down
And sniff the beautiful flowers.

If I had wings
I would lay down in the grass
And it would tickle my feet and toes.

If I had wings
I would seek the birds while they swoop down at the grass
And try to get some worms that wriggle.

Jenna McGlade (7)
Hampton Junior School

WINGS

If I had wings
I would twirl with the birds

If I had wings
I would wake to the calling birds and the chirruping robin

If I had wings
I would scoop up the vanilla ice cream from the glittering moon

If I had wings
I would dance under the rainbow

If I had wings
I would glide with the jewelled butterflies

If I had wings
I would glide with the birds.

Alexandra Thomas (7)
Hampton Junior School

MY PUPPY

My puppy is an active puppy
His name is Max.
He's always chewing my toys.
He's almost like a barking dustbin.
Max eats everything he sees,
He's always eating my dinner with those cute eyes.
My puppy, Max, is playful as ever.
Every time Max hears his lead rattle
He's up in a dash and jumps around me
And runs round the house like a mad thing.
When I walk Max he is playful with everyone and everything.

Lauren Benham (10)
Lavender Primary School

YOU CAN GIVE UP AS MANY TIMES AS YOU LIKE AS LONG AS YOUR FEET KEEP MOVING

It took an hour to reach the bottom
Then I realised it was a mistake
Any enjoyment at all was forgotten
I wondered how long it would take
The top was high and covered with clouds
I looked at it in dismay
My attempts to block out the pain had failed
It was going to be a long day
Halfway up and halfway dead
I felt I could walk no more
I didn't have the energy to lift my head
And have a vivid view of the floor
To my left was a vertical drop
Straight down the side of the mountain
And because I was so far from the top
Down looked very inviting.

Emily Gonella (10)
Lavender Primary School

RICH AND POOR

We have houses and spectate
But they are hungry and migrate
They are begging on the streets
We are warm, eating sweets
They are searching through the bins
We are eating out of tins
They are sleeping covered in fleas
But we sleep comfortably as we please
From the poor one has chanted
'The rich takes us all for granted.'

Jedakiah Simonenko (10)
Lavender Primary School

THE MAN

The man I used to know
Was my best neighbour, not.
His habits always got on my nerves.
Move this, move that, every day
And time to Hoover, time to dust.
One day I came home to watch the man
But all throughout the week
He wasn't there.
I asked my mum,
She said, 'Don't worry, he's on holiday I suppose.'
Other than that my mum stopped to say, 'Hello,' to my neighbour.
She asked what was wrong.
She said, 'You know that man you know?
When you were away he was killed by someone we know . . .'

Amber Prendergast (11)
Lavender Primary School

THE MOUSE

Creeping quietly along the squeaky floor,
He's only found a few crumbs but desperately wants more!

He hopes that he will not see the family's cat,
For the cat might eat him and then he'd be fat.

The cat has awoken and is walking down the hall,
The mouse scuttles away, he's climbing up the wall!

The cat is now hungry, he wants to fill his tum,
He pounces upon the mouse, gulp, purr, yum, yum!

Hannah Elizabeth Barnes (10)
Lavender Primary School

COLOURS

Blue is the water flowing on by
Blue is the colour of the skies up high

Yellow is the sun that brightens up the land
Yellow is the colour of the sand

Red is the flames hot and bright
Red is the faces of kids in a fight

Green is the grass, stealthy and short
Green are the grapes, they're my sort

Pink are the pigs, cute and fat
Pink is the tail of a rat

Colours are lovely, bright and bold
In steaming hot times or in the cold
You see colours night and day
Our world is bright and never grey.

Jessica Parks & Maisie Sims (11)
Lavender Primary School

THE CAT AND THE MOUSE

The cat spotted a mouse,
On a rainy day,
The cat spotted a mouse,
Whose birthday is in May,
The cat liked to tease,
The mouse liked cheese,
The cat ate the mouse,
Then went back to his cosy house.

Nicola Disney (9)
Lavender Primary School

THE ANIMAL WORLD!

1 fat pig, snorting down the road,
Along comes a chicken,
Hugging a little toad.
2 smelly rats, wandering around the bins.
3 black bats, scratching the metal tins.
4 blue whales, squirting water,
Along comes a genius divide them into a quarter.
Then when they go home,
They found a goose alone.
Then along came a farmer, dressed all in his armour!
When he comes up the yard,
He finds his old birthday card.
They all go to sleep
And wake up to find a dead sheep.
When they all get up
They find birds nibbling on cups
And the animals come along
To sing a funny song.

Tia Ranaldi & Masie Sims (9)
Lavender Primary School

NOISE POEM

The stairs of the steeple
The noises of the people
Miaowing of the cat
The treading on a mat
The cutting of the scissors
And the noise of the lizards.

Ellis Cook (10)
Lavender Primary School

DOLPHINS

Dolphins splash
In the ocean

The dolphin has such
A gentle motion

They are friendly
Also clever

One of the prettiest
Creatures ever

Dolphins eat fish
They think it is
A tasty dish.

Katie McDonnell (10)
Lavender Primary School

ZOO

Once I went to the zoo
And saw a kangaroo.
There were loads and loads of monkeys
Who were playing with toy donkeys.
I also saw some bears
Who had not paid for their fares.
Best of all I saw a lion
Who swallowed a boy called Ryan.
Finally I saw a seal
Who had made an excellent deal.

Priscilla Mahendran (10)
Lavender Primary School

POLLUTION

The air's full of pollution and dust,
From things we do for fun,
Not things we must.

The air's full of carbon and lead,
That makes things ill
And sometimes dead.

The air's full of smog and gas,
Using oil and petrol
To the max.

The air should be clean, fresh and light,
All the time,
Day and night.

Richard Stephens (10)
Lavender Primary School

DISCO CITY

It's getting dark in Disco City,
The lights are turning on.
The people are looking very pretty,
Dancing to the disco song.

It really, really is a pity,
That the people outside are gone.
The people on the dance floor are very witty,
For dancing to the disco song.

Kelly Smyth (10)
Lavender Primary School

WHY IS IT?

Why is it?
Why is it that she gets that?
Why is it that he gets that?
Why is it that I don't?
Why? Why? Why?

Why is it?
Why is it that she has a friend?
Why is it that he has a friend?
Why is it that I don't?
Why? Why? Why?

Why is it?
Why is it that she plays?
Why is it that he plays?
Why is it that I don't?
Why? Why? Why?

Why is it?
Why is it that she gets a prize?
Why is it that he gets a prize?
Why is it that I don't?
Why? Why? Why?

Amintha Ballard (10)
Lavender Primary School

CHOCOLATE

Chocolate I love you.
Chocolate I care.
Chocolate is yummy.
Chocolate eclairs.

Chocolate is lovely.
Chocolate is sweet.
Chocolate you're wonderful.
You're all I want to eat.

Poppy Manze (10)
Lavender Primary School

YOU CAN DO IT!

You can lift a weight if you're big and strong,
You can play a flute which is silver and long.

You can build houses in a long row,
You can make the rooms small and the ceilings low.

You can bake a cake, chocolate and toffee!
You can make it taste nice by having it with coffee!

You can play Monopoly if you dare!
Or you can play Snakes and Ladders as a pair.

You can work in an office, I'm sure you'll be proud,
Or you can be a cook to serve the crowd.

I'm sure you can do something, like be an artist,
You can be a pianist, I'm sure you'll be the smartest!

You can do anything,
And you can do something.
You can't do nothing,
You can do everything!

Matthew Anastasis (10)
Lavender Primary School

TIME

I awake in the morning,
I look at my clock,
It's very early,
It's seven o'clock.

I'm ready for school,
I'm making my way,
Oh no, I forgot,
It's Saturday.

I'm getting my tracksuit bottoms on,
I've taken half an hour,
I'm going to a party in a minute,
I still need to have a shower.

I'm really, really late,
Not a minute to spare,
Where are my shoes?
I need to brush my hair.

Rhian Goddard (10)
Lavender Primary School

THE SHEEP

One dark night when I couldn't sleep
My mum said, 'Why don't you try counting sheep?'
Lying, staring at the sky I thought, 'Why not give it a try?'

One sheep, two sheep, three sheep . . .
Loads of sheep later . . .
'Mum! Mum! I still can't sleep.'
'Never mind, darling. Bah! Bah,' she bleated.

Lauren Bacon (11)
Lavender Primary School

MY TEACHER

My teacher is nice and snappy
She looks like an elephant
And stinks like a nappy.
She has hair like a monkey
And teeth like the big, bad wolf.
She has arms like a gorilla
And legs like a cat
A nose like a fish
And a mouth like a rat.
Her mouth is so big
She cannot close it.
She has a brain like a dog
And a belly button like a feather
And there is white fluff inside.
She has ears so big
They're as big as people
And eyes as big and blue
As a bumblebee.

Amy Slater (10)
Lavender Primary School

MR LOULETTE

There was once a man called Mr Loulette
He thought he would win some money by playing roulette
But all he won
Was a packet of gum
And never played roulette again.

Bradley John O'Brien (10)
Lavender Primary School

THE ERASING WORLD

I saw a man
With an enormous eraser.
He came to town
And he erased
The cars,
The shops,
The roads,
The birds,
Even the town.
He left me alone
With nothing
But the colour
White.

Ajantha Ballard (10)
Lavender Primary School

PIGS CAN FLY

'Pigs can fly,' said Pig to Cow.
'Prove it then and show me how.'
So up Pig went, up to the sky,
'See, I told you pigs can fly.'
So off Pig flew, above the trees,
Over the oceans and the seas.
He went to Germany, France and Spain,
Through the sun and through the rain.
He flew on and on through stormy nights,
Till he finished his long, long flight.
But then a man inside New York,
Turned dear old Pig to roasted pork.

Aisling Marie Burrell (10)
Our Lady & St John's School

CHARLOTTE

My mummy bought me a hamster
We had to buy a cage
I chose a blue one with small bars
Because of her young age

I bought her from Silvesters
The top cage on the right
When the cutest face caught my eye
It was true love at first sight

Her fur was long and fluffy
All brown and cream and white
Her eyes they shone like shining stars
Oh she was my delight!

Charlotte loves her food
All the lovely sweets
Honey-sticks and wafers
And all the chocolate treats

Because she loves her food so much
And isn't quite so small
She needs to do some exercise
In her running ball

Her little face looks forward
Her cute paws on the ball
Shooting across the wooden floor
Without a care at all

And when it is time for bed
She snuggles into a ball
In her cosy, little house
Filled with cotton wool.

Florence Hannon (10)
Our Lady & St John's School

BIG NICKY THE BEAR

I once had a bear
It was a marvellous toy.
When I was smaller
It gave me bundles of joy.
Its paws were all sticky
Its one eye looked ever so tricky
And I named him Big Nicky The Bear.
Wherever I went
He was there at my side,
Smiling away with enormous pride.

But along came my brother
With a boy called Glover
And they took Big Nicky away.
They sprinted to a field
As I told them, 'Yield,'
But they pushed me aside and ran.
That's when my troubles began.

Then I got a letter
Which made me feel better,
It was from Big Nicky The Bear.
He said he was in Chicago
With his cousin Margo
And soon he'll be out of there.

A month later I heard a knock at the door
And through the letterbox Big Nicky fell to the floor.
I picked him up and held him tight,
Now I'll never let him out of my sight.
I love my bear
With his chocolate-coloured hair.
He's back, he's back, Big Nicky The Bear.

Thomas Jewers (11)
Our Lady & St John's School

FOOTBALL TEAMS

Man United are the best
Simply better than all the rest
They have the skill, they have the pace
But they don't know how to tie a lace.

Chelsea, Chelsea have the skill
Zola's shot could definitely kill
They have the English, they have French
But some of them are on the bench.

Arsenal have the players and also the kit
But they do a super hit
They have red cards and yellow too
Sometimes they do miss the cue.

Liverpool have Owen and also Gerrard
Sometimes their opponents are really hard
They wear red like Man U do
But they wear green sometimes too.

Brentford stand out, that's where I live
They like to share, they like to give
They are quick, good but not the best
Division Two is their nest.

Hanwell Town is where I play
I have a match every Sunday
We wear black and white, the strip is new
We need support, can you help too?

Joe Smith (10)
Our Lady & St John's School

HAVE YOU EVER . . .

Have you ever seen the glow of a star
So gold and bright?
Have you seen its gleaming shimmer,
In the dark of night?

Have you ever heard the song
Of a robin so small and sweet?
Have you seen it show-off its red breast
Whilst singing: tweet, tweet, tweet?

Have you ever smelled the fragrance
Of a rose so rosy red
In the middle of an amazing,
Colourful flower bed?

Have you ever experienced these things?
Just remember what I've said.

Clare Friel (10)
Our Lady & St John's School

UNDER THE SEA

Deep, deep down in the sea,
Where the dolphins flee,
When sharks are near,
The fish are filled with fear.

Deep, deep under the boats,
The divers are raising their hopes,
Some treasure lays down there
But you must treat it with care.

'It's here, it's here.'
The fish shook with fear,
For anyone who opens the chest,
Will be a big, big pest.

Aran Mullarkey (10)
Our Lady & St John's School

MICHAEL JACKSON

Why does everyone hate him?
He's really not that bad,
Just because he's famous,
People try to make him sad.

If he was just plain rubbish,
Then try and tell me this,
Why he gets so many Grammies,
And why his songs still stick.

People call him all sorts of names,
But who are they to judge?
Though he tries to give us pleasure,
They will always hold a grudge.

Take me as an example,
That not everyone goes with the groove,
I want you to answer this question,
As long as you tell me the truth.

Do you believe he's rubbish?
Do you believe he's great?
I will leave you with your party,
To discuss and participate.

Keyan Salarkia (11)
Our Lady & St John's School

THE DARKNESS . . .

I was lying in the darkness,
When a thought soared into my mind,
If only I could fly like a bird,
And leave the world behind.

I was lying in the darkness,
When a thought floated into my head,
If only I could swim like a fish,
Cruising by miles ahead.

I was lying in the darkness,
When a thought stuck my brain,
If only I could gallop like a horse,
With the wind blowing through my mane.

I was lying in the darkness,
When a thought came to me,
If only I could help people in pain,
What a wonderful person I would be.

Rhea Chandler (11)
Our Lady & St John's School

MY TREASURE

My treasure, my treasure, my wonderful treasure
You are a talent which I have
I love you, I love you, my beautiful treasure
Because of you I am like my friend Dave

You're to do with a tune, a tune on an instrument
It's not like a drum or a piano
It is an instrument much like a cello
The strings vibrate much like a double bass
But I go sailing through my grades

It has four sizes, ¼, ½, ¾, 1 whole
It is as light as air
And you put it on your shoulder
It is a violin, a wonderful violin.

Andre Yeghiazarian (11)
Our Lady & St John's School

CHILDHOOD

Childhood is fun
Childhood is happy
It is a time for excitement
It is a time for new things

Childhood is exciting
Childhood is playful
It is a time to be friendly
It is a time for fun and games

Childhood is a time to enjoy
Childhood is a time to grow up
It is a time for activities
It is a time for happiness

Childhood is a time for school
Childhood is a time to learn
It is a time to learn new subjects
It is a time to have new friends.

Ari Boghosian (10)
Our Lady & St John's School

ANYTHING

I'm sitting at my desk just scrawling,
The homework Miss set tonight is appalling,
To write a poem on anything,
On any subject at all,
'It could rhyme or not,' she said,
'The choice is yours,' she said.

Write about what? I thought and I thought,
That I ended up feeling rather distraught,
Trying to remember all the rules that I was taught.

Boys always write about rockets and cars,
And end up talking about their favourite, famous, football stars,
I could write about school,
But that wouldn't be cool,
The others would laugh,
And I'd feel like a fool.
Girls always write about doing their make-up and hair,
Where as I don't really give a care.

This poem is all that worries me,
Because I don't know what to write, you see.
Perhaps when I look I'm over and done,
Just when I thought I hadn't begun,
So let's not pretend
I've come to *the end.*

Georgina Butler (10)
Our Lady & St John's School

DEATH

Death is cruel, why does it happen?
Your life on Earth ends in a coffin.
All the questions going round in your head,
We'll know the answers when we're dead.

It sometimes happens sooner rather than later,
But in the end it's all down to fate.
But for now life we must live,
To love all others and to forget and forgive.

Leon Chandiram (10)
Our Lady & St John's School

COVER FROM THE STORM

There was an old man aged seventy or so,
Plodding along swiftly he would go.
With the only family member he had left,
All the others had climbed the heavenly steps.

His grandson skipping whilst clapping his hands,
The tide coming in revealing footsteps on the sand.
Up they climbed the sandy stairs,
Until they reached the city's polluted air.
Crossing the road hand in hand,
Thinking about dinner plans.

Mother Nature's baby started bawling,
Yes, that's right, the rain started falling.
The rain broke into a dark storm,
And they decided to take cover from it all.

Down they went a dark, lonely, back street,
Beginning to hear more than two pairs of feet.
The petrified boy turned around with a tear in his eye,
He suddenly began to scream and cry.

'The boy's going to die now!' a dark voice said,
The elderly man turned around,
'No, take me instead!'

Nicole Serdet (11)
Our Lady & St John's School

UP IN THE SKY

Up in the sky there is so much to see,
The sun, the moon and me.
I live in the sky, up with the stars,
Up with Venus and Mars.
All up in the sky.

Up in the sky there are clouds that are white,
Grey ones and black ones which give you a fright.
Lightning, snow, hail and rain,
All for me to control and sustain.
All up in the sky.

Some days are hot, some are cold,
Some are in-between, so I've been told.
Planes pass by, choppers and all,
The tops of buildings, so high and tall.
All up in the sky.

Up in the sky there is so much to see,
The sun, the moon and me.

Jason Daniel Gouveia Law (10)
Our Lady & St John's School

WAR

War means death, war is sad,
Lifeless bodies, nor good, nor bad.
Fighting for freedom or for fun,
There's no turning back, what's done is done.
Metal bullets fly trough the air,
If you're shot no one will care.
There you lie on the ground,
Motionless bodies all around.

What will happen to your families now?
They'll wonder why and how.
After a few days you begin to rise,
Up to Heaven where no one dies.
Hundreds of graves are built for those,
Who fought for us and never rose.
So up they go to paradise now,
Instead of crying they'll say, 'Wow.'

Richard Hugo Cole (11)
Our Lady & St John's School

SOLDIER

Soldier, soldier on the floor,
You joined this war,
But you're not here anymore.
As they choke, look down on your grave,
I thank God for moving you away from the gore.
Your army and friends think, 'Why such a young age,
What a brave soldier I saw.'

Some wars take quite some time to end, for them,
We'll send peacemaking troops and friends.

Some soldiers may not die thanks to them who 'body mend'.
But some are under the ground from the bombing,
They're never found.

Their souls are in Heaven, high up, safe and sound.
From me to you, friends, army and family,
I'm high up in the sky,
So friends, army and family

Goodbye.

Daniel Day (11)
Our Lady & St John's School

DOLLY THE DOLPHIN

Dolly the dolphin loved to sit on her mum's lap,
Always playing in the sea without the aid of a map,
Looking for adventure every step of the way,
Out at night and in the day.

Friends of hers were the ones to see,
Jumping around and bouncing with glee,
Molly, Holly and don't forget Elly the Jelly,
She's the one with the big, fat belly. (Jellyfish)

Adventure by day,
And by night,
The gang together,
Are a really great sight.

Dolphin and her pals,
All agreed,
That one day she'll make a tale,
For us to read.

Jessica Bondzie (11)
Our Lady & St John's School

SUN

The sun was bright in the boiling sky.
It had lots of big flashes like Mum's home-made pie.
It could be filled with apples or strawberries and cream.
Oh boy it's so boiling, with such a bright beam.

It looked like a big bright, yellow ball,
Or maybe a big, yellow balloon up high and tall.
It could be a monkey with bright, yellow spots,
Or maybe a tiger with yellow polka dots.

Maybe a cookie with white chocolate drops,
Or maybe some sand with a few snowdrops.
It could be a lemon or an iced bun,
But no, it's just the plain old sun.

Phoebe McCullough (10)
Our Lady & St John's School

HIDDEN TREASURE

The scorching hot sand is burning my feet,
My face is pouring with sweat from this oh so hot heat.
The treasure must not be far away now,
But how will we reach it oh how, oh how?
Most of my family are walking with pride,
It's as if they're taking one big stride.
Suddenly there is a call from my intelligent dad,
'We have reached the treasure, oh we have, we have!
All we have to do is start digging here
And as we dig deeper the treasure should appear.'
So then and there we picked up our spades
And started to work very hard like housemaids.
Time went on, it was four hours later
And when we looked up the darkness grew greater.
But as luck would have it we had found our main prize,
And, looking into Heaven, we all closed our eyes.
Immediately Uncle Tom lifted the box out,
Then he got the key without a doubt.
Our eyes then opened and we looked inside the chest,
But all there was, was a dirty, blue vest.
We've come all this way
And now all I can say
Is I hope you've enjoyed listening about my very long day!

Caitlin Murphy (10)
Our Lady & St John's School

My Brother

My brother is a little boy.
Bob the Builder is his favourite toy.
He takes him wherever he goes,
Through rain, sun or winter snow.
He watches Playdays and says,
'What stop will it be today?'
Sometimes he goes to the park
And hears dogs bark.
He will break a vase one day
And walk away.
Mum and Dad try to play
But they get pushed away
And now it's time for bed
So night, night sleepyhead.

Curtis Hoogwerf (10)
Our Lady & St John's School

Mr Spider

Mr Spider creeps about, especially at night.
Once your mum has tucked you in and turned off the light.
He scuttles round for bits and pieces,
Left in the rubbish bin for Mr Spider's tea.
Then he runs to the bathroom for a little were.
He says to himself, 'No doubt, not doubt
I will make this family scream and shout.
I'll jump in the bath
And have a bit of a laugh
But how will they react?
They made me pack and sent me away
But they haven't got rid of me
Naa, not that easily.'

Cal Freire (11)
Our Lady & St John's School

THE SUN

The sun is coming out today with a smiling face,
He's coming out to play with the human race.

He loves to play with his friends,
And shine on their Mercedes-Benz.

The sun is nice, big and bright,
He gives his playmates lots of lovely light.

He's polite, he's nice,
He's like sugar and spice.

He's like a candle for an outside diner,
He shines on those who eat in China.

But for now, it's time to rest
So that in the morning he will look his best.

Rosie Murphy (10)
Our Lady & St John's School

STORMY

It is a dark and windy day.
We splash in the puddles.
We put up our colourful umbrellas.
The clouds are dull.
The thunder crashes.
The lightning flashes.
We run inside, we are very wet.
The stormy clouds are going away.
It looks like it is going to be a nice day.

Adam Jary (8)
Royal National Orthopaedic Hospital

CANDLE

C hristmas candles light the tree
A re those presents all for me?
N o! They're for everyone so
D on't go opening them all.
L ook the candles are burning bright
E very one, a beautiful sight.

Michaela Durgan (10)
Royal National Orthopaedic Hospital

OUR FAVOURITE SEASON OF THE YEAR

Buzzing bees making honey
Tweeting birds making nests
Sunflowers gently blowing in the breeze
Let's go and see the green trees.

Nadia Benabdellah & Benjamin Duke (9)
Royal National Orthopaedic Hospital

CANDLE

C andles
A re
N ice for
D ecorating the
L iving room
E specially at Christmas.

Joshua Hodges (6)
Royal National Orthopaedic Hospital

GOAL!

I walk onto the field
Dressed in red and blue
It's about to start
Right on cue

I hear the shouts
Of the screaming crowd
I will do something
Of which to be proud

The whistle blows
Off go the teams
This is the moment
That comes in my dreams

My team-mate runs
Down the pitch
But then occurs
A slight hitch

'Penalty!' we cry
The ref points to the spot
My hands are shaking
My face is red-hot

I run to the ball
The crowd roared
It hits the net
I've scored!

Andrew Dallal (11)
St Christopher's Prep School

THE FOREST

As I walk through the forest,
I can see birds flying in the sky.
I can see monkeys swinging from tree to tree as they chatter,
I can see leopards climbing trees and lying on them.
As I get nearer to the lake,
I can see crocodiles and alligators.
I can see the cheetah coming,
From where I am crouching I can watch him pounce on his prey.
As I walk further into the forest,
I can see the panther,
Creeping through the grass
And the lion close behind.
I get more and more frightened and scared
But there is no need because I know Jesus is near.

Edmund Norris (9)
St Christopher's Prep School

DEEP, DARK CAVE

Let's go into the deep, dark cave.
   'Beware', it says.
It's dark and spooky.
   We have no light.
I hear a roar! We're all scared.
   It's fine. It's far away, we will be safe.
But no one knows who lives in there.
   We go to sleep and find something soft.
It starts to move. I am the only one awake.
   Then . . . we jump up and scream while running!
We are running so fast we fall into the stream
   And are never to be seen again.

Rebecca English (9)
St Christopher's Prep School

THE FOUR MEN

There was a man called Bruno
Who went for a . . . u know,
He took a long time
And lost a dime
And that was the man called Bruno.

There was a man called José
Who went far, far away,
The seas he crossed
Made him totally lost
And that was the man called José.

There was a man called Sam
Who lived near a dam.
He did not like it there
Cos he lived with a bear
And that was the man called Sam.

There was a man called Owen
Who loved to do sewin',
He would sew and sew all day
Oh he did get carried away
And that was the man called Owen.

Now Bruno, Owen, José and Sam
Went to an island called 'Sunny Japan'.
It was there that they awoke
In the middle of the night,
To the sound of a dragon,
Which gave them a fright.

The hairs on their necks all stood on ends,
For fear they might lose one of their friends.

Louisa Worley (11)
St Christopher's Prep School

IN THE WOODS

I'm in the woods,
I hear rustling beside me.
I hear owls above and mice below,
I see big shadows which are trees.
I run around,
I cry for help,
Hoping to be found.
The stars are bright,
The moon is shining.
I think I hear people,
But it's the wind whining.
I wish I hadn't run away.
I wonder what my mum will say?
Then suddenly a big creature leaps out!
I scream, I shout!
It's sniffing my leg.
I see something.
It's an orange snout.
I try to touch, but it runs away.
I'm tired, I go to sleep, I sleep in peace.
Then it seems something's touching me.
I wake up and see - the police.
They take me to my house.
I think I like it more at home
Than being in the woods alone.

Spencer Zen Richards (10)
St Christopher's Prep School

THE RIVER

Through the valley, the rushing river streams,
Bluey-green swirls ripple.
The small boat moves rapidly along,
Carrying a poor little fisherman to the sea.

The streaming water trickles down the waterfall,
Turning into a sea of colour.
The river flows on, starting to overflow,
Creeping gently . . . gently . . . gently onto the bank.

Jessica Lancod-Frost (9)
St Christopher's Prep School

SWEET SHOP

Round the corner,
Children run to Tony's sweet shop.

They look inside,
So many kinds,
Yellow, pink, green with blue spots.

Children running around,
Trying to find Wonker Bars with the six golden tickets.

Look there! Look where?
Just underneath that shelf!

Tony's put out the rainbow pop star candy.
My sister got Kylie Minogue.
I want that girl from S Club 7.

Oh no! Here comes Sharon!
Let's get those sweets quickly
Before she takes them!

'60p for you and 20p for you!
Do you all want those pop stars candies?

Take them all then.'
'Thank you, Tony!'

Serena Patel (10)
St Christopher's Prep School

THE LEOPARD

As I stroll in the deep, dark frost,
I see a bloodthirsty leopard chasing its terrified prey.
The brown ink pools on its silky skin,
Shaped like dripping raindrops.
As it creeps along the twiggy ground,
Low and sharp it hunts.
It leaps like a jumping frog but misses.
The antelope is running for its life.
The sound from the cracking twigs are like bones snapping.
The panting of the antelope is like a heart
Breathing a thousand times faster than it should.
Silence!
It was finished and all I saw were two green traffic lights
Glaring at me . . .

Nicholas Demetriou (11)
St Christopher's Prep School

MY MOTHER

When she sings she's like a train on fire,
Her curly hair and large mouth mean something dire,
She's an opera singer, you should know,
She opens her mouth with a terrifying blow.
The songs she can sing fill the church with noise,
When she talks on the phone, it even scares boys!

Her massive figure barges through crowds,
Her stomach loves food - she can eat mounds,
She may sound dumb,
But not to me,
And that's because,
She's my mum!

Daniel Ong (10)
St Christopher's Prep School

THE DEEPER YOU GO . . .

The deeper you go . . .
You've got to remember that
Even an otter knows
Because . . .
The otter dives . . .
Lands in the water with no sound at all,
But you do see ripples and then no more.
The otter swims deeper,
Gliding all the way.
A fish passes,
But the otter does not try to get that fish.
Because he knows the deeper you go . . .
Swiftly he swims, bit by bit, deeper.
Determinedly and gracefully,
Has his battle with the water,
Fighting, so as not to be pulled to the surface.
Going deeper . . . and deeper . . .
Then, achieving his goal,
Gets deep enough,
And there, are more fish than ever at the surface.
When he's caught his fish
He swims back the way he came,
And suddenly bursts to the surface,
Then jumps on land,
And shakes his silky, shiny fur then eats . . .
See, he knows . . .
The deeper you go the more you find . . .

Emily Smith (10)
St Christopher's Prep School

DOWNHILL

The sun is shining,
The snow is gleaming,
The lifts are climbing,
The slopes are teeming.

My heart is racing,
My skis are gliding,
My friends are chasing,
There is no hiding.

I'm skidding through the snow,
Getting faster as I go.
I'm going through the trees,
Getting weaker in my knees.

It's starting to snow,
But there's not much further to go.
It's the end of a beautiful day,
And there is nothing more to say.

Adrian McBride (10)
St Christopher's Prep School

THE TIGER

As it crept through the grass
Animals let him stride past.
Suddenly he sees his prey
I know, I saw it gently sway.

The tiger was orange and black
He was ready for the attack.
The prey jumped back in fear
For the tiger was getting too near.

The prey fell to the floor
It looked ever so sore.
The tiger took it away
I feel sorry for this poor little prey.

Flora Kupfer (11)
St Christopher's Prep School

QUIDDITCH

I run onto the pitch,
The crowd are screaming.
I can see how big the pitch is.
I mount my broomstick,
As everyone else does.
The referee blows her whistle.

I kick-off off the ground.
As I soar,
Into the clear blue sky,
I can feel the air on my face.

Suddenly I see a glimpse of gold,
Against the horizon.
I put on a burst of speed,
As a Bludger skims my ear.

I see the glimpse of gold,
More clearly now,
Right in front of me.
I stretch out my hand . . .

There is a vibration,
In my hand.
I've caught the Snitch!

Sam Tuchband (11)
St Christopher's Prep School

TREASURE AT SEA

There's treasure at sea
But where can it be?
It glitters and shines
And it is all mine.
I will cross the seven seas
Even if it takes ten years.
I will find the island
And dig and dig but when my shovel breaks
I shall find a lake.
I fish for kippers for tea
Make myself a hut
But I soon feel parched
So it's not gold I want . . . it's water!

Molly Campbell (9)
St Christopher's Prep School

DIFFERENT DIMENSIONS

Open the door and you will see . . .
A haunted house, with the ghostly three,
One of them had stinky breath
Another had a nasty death!

There's a sissy place in outer space
Where fairies spin in the dark blue sky.
Now say goodbye, goodbye!

The tropical forest, get tangled in vines
Sorry, there is no wine, there are tigers,
Monkeys who are very funky!

Let's stop dreaming!

William Kupfer (11)
St Christopher's Prep School

THE DRAGON

The knight
Walked towards
The dragon and
Drew his sword.
The dragon
Blew fire and
The knight
Stood back.
Then the
Dragon stamped
Towards him
A bit more.
Very quickly
The dragon
Tried to grab
Him, but missed.
So the dragon
Tried again,
But it was too
Late; the knight
Had already
Stabbed him
And the
Dragon collapsed
Dead!

Nicole Smallman (9)
St Christopher's Prep School

THE RAINFOREST

Eagles screeching high,
Gliding through the pinky, orange, horizon sky.

The elegant movement of the jet-black panther,
Concentrating on its daily prey.

The rushing of the rapid water in the distance,
Showering over the crowded rocks.

The energetic monkeys swinging from branch to branch,
And tree to tree, swaying to and fro.

Pearly dewdrops on my pale, soft skin,
Which trickle me and make me grin.

The camouflaged snakes slithering,
On the luscious green.

Reeya Patel (10)
St Christopher's Prep School

THE FOOTBALL MATCH

I hear the cheering of the crowds as the match begins
The players run out onto the pitch
And line up as if they were statues
I hear the shrill sound of the whistle as the match begins
The players run around frantically looking for a pass
The ball leaps into the air
Suddenly the ball drops
The referee blows his whistle
The crowd erupts like a volcano
We've won!

Simran Lotay (10)
St Christopher's Prep School

THE STRANGE WITCH

She didn't see me hiding, behind an ivy bush,
Until my friend starts sneezing, *aichoo!*

I ran, I hid, she caught me however
And threw me into a cave, as hard as she could!

I cried, I wept, I begged and pleaded,
However hard I tried, she never changed her mind.

Then she grabbed me by my arm,
Threw me out the door,
Got her cat to scratch me, with its sharp claws!

I screamed, I howled but no one came,
To help me with first aid!

I think that taught me a lesson, not to mess about,
With cruel, mean witches,
Like the witch who nearly ate me!

Kanchana Harendran (9)
St Christopher's Prep School

MY BEST FRIEND CALLED STEPHANIE

My best friend called Stephanie is really my best friend.
We tell each other secrets and play round the bed.

My best friend called Stephanie is really my best friend.
We laugh together and play with no end.

We get up to mischief lots of times
The we laugh and giggle and be surprised.

Kathryn Crockford (9)
St Ignatius RC Primary School, Sunbury-on-Thames

WHAT IS BLUE?

Blue is new
Blue can be a dark, night sky
Blue is a stream
Which flows non-stop
Blue is a pencil
Blue is a book
Blue is a box
Which is used every day
Blue is totally like a dream
Blue is a chair,
Blue is a tray
Blue can see an X-ray
Blue is the best
But the wrong seen colour
For an arm in the leg.

Stephen Costa (9)
St Ignatius RC Primary School, Sunbury-on-Thames

WHAT IS GREEN?

The grass was green
When I was in class.

The leaves of trees
Are so very green
When the hummingbirds sing
A happy song

Irish shamrocks
Can be green
If you are very, very keen.

Danielle Goody (9)
St Ignatius RC Primary School, Sunbury-on-Thames

UNDER THE OCEAN

When I was under the ocean
Sent to look for a potion
The ocean was dark and gloomy
And deep, I found a potion that I would keep
I saw a chest, it was a mess
I opened the box,
There was a couple of rags and sock
I opened the sock
It had something inside it
I think someone has been hiding it.
I drank some potion
It made me dizzy
But, mind you,
The potion was fizzy.

James Crouchman (9)
St Ignatius RC Primary School, Sunbury-on-Thames

TEDDY TREASURE

In a dark, dark room
Somewhere was a teddy
A boy came up and took it down the stairs
Suddenly he heard something rattle
It fell on the chairs, he was amazed!
He saw a hole and looked inside
He saw jewels upon jewels and shining gold
He'd found a hidden treasure
He kept it safe and sound.

Alexandar Francis-Lynch (10)
St Ignatius RC Primary School, Sunbury-on-Thames

WHAT IS BLUE?

Blue is the water, blue is the sky,
Blue is the twinkle
That shines in my eye.
Blue is some paper, blue is a box,
Blue is the water
That comes from a fox.

Blue is a river, blue is a stream,
Blue is totally like a dream.
Blue is a chair, blue is a tray,
Blue can see in an X-ray.

Blue is the *best,* blue is good
But it's not the right colour
For a plank of wood . . .

Max England (8)
St Ignatius RC Primary School, Sunbury-on-Thames

WHAT IS YELLOW?

Yellow is the sun shining high
Yellow is the sun having fun
Yellow is the daffodils having fun
In the sun all day long.

Yellow is like a golden hen
Yellow is honey that bears eat
Yellow is the moon shining high
Yellow is a peg that says your age
Yellow is the golden sand
Yellow is an arrow pointing south
Yellow is a tag that says your name.

Danielle Armstrong (8)
St Ignatius RC Primary School, Sunbury-on-Thames

I FOUND IT IN THE PLAYGROUND

I found it in the playground
The playground
The playground
I found it in the playground
In a very small box
I dug, I dug
To try and get it out
I dug, I dug
To try and get it out
There's a map in the box
There's a map in the box
There a map, a map, a map in the box
What shall I do?
What shall I do?
What shall I
What shall I
What shall I do?
I am going to follow the map
The map
The map
I am going to follow the map to the treasure
Now I have found the treasure I am full of pleasure.

Chris Bootle (10)
St Ignatius RC Primary School, Sunbury-on-Thames

VAMPIRES

I saw a vampire in my room
He looked all old and his teeth were too
He flew out of my window like a bat
And as he went I said,
'Beware and beware of the dead.'

Jorja Suchodolska (9)
St Ignatius RC Primary School, Sunbury-on-Thames

DEAD MAN'S CURSE

I have found a hole,
In it I do not know what will be,
It might be a dead man's soul.

I am starting to dig,
I have found a box,
It is very big.

I can feel the wind blowing my coat,
I have got the box open,
In it is a note.

I have fallen over, it could be worse,
The note says:
'Any man that reads this will be . . .
Cursed.'

Ryan Frank Hill (10)
St Ignatius RC Primary School, Sunbury-on-Thames

HORRIBLE HOMEWORK

Moody maths,
Lame literacy,
Sleepy science,
Hated history,
Dodgy DT,
Rubbish RE.

But the best thing is
Every Friday
We go to the swimming pool!

I hate
Homework!

Rosie Thurgood (9)
St Ignatius RC Primary School, Sunbury-on-Thames

WHAT IS BLUE?

The blue sky
Is so very bright
With powdery clouds so very white.

Blue is a flower
So soft and sour
And full of energetic power.

Blue is the ocean
So very deep
When it stays still it's having a sleep.

Blue is a pair of eyes
Staring at you
Waiting for your replies.

Blue is a colour
I love so much

I love blue!

Holly Thornton (9)
St Ignatius RC Primary School, Sunbury-on-Thames

SAND IN YOUR SANDWICHES

Seeing the sea is *fun*
Seeing the crabs is scary
Seeing the fish is fun
Seeing the boats bouncing
I like ice cream
I like sandcastles
I like looking for shells
I don't like sand in my sandwiches.

Joseph Hood (8)
St Ignatius RC Primary School, Sunbury-on-Thames

TREASURE UNDER THE SEA

It's a clear, sunny morning
I'm going for a swim
I hope I see lots of dolphins
With pointy fins.

I climb out of the boat into the clear, warm water
I see my friend fishing
Her name is Emma Porter.

I go deeper and deeper and it gets scarier and scarier
And blarier and blarier
It's getting really dark
What's that swimming towards me?
Is it a a a a shark?

No, only a friendly dolphin
I quite like it too.

I feel full of pleasure
I've just found some treasure
What shall I do?

I swim up to the surface
The sun shines on my hair
The dolphin comes up to say goodbye
It looks as if it doesn't have a care!

Sophie Ann Perez (10)
St Ignatius RC Primary School, Sunbury-on-Thames

WHAT IS BLACK?

Black is for grunge, gothic and punk.
Gothics wear black lipstick and nail varnish.
Punks totally like black and like to play with junk.
Grungers like black because it can start and finish.

Black is a spider waiting for its prey.
Black is a jacket people like to wear.
Black is an ant having a great day.
Black is a colour that gives you a dare.

Jordan Chandramohan (9)
St Ignatius RC Primary School, Sunbury-on-Thames

HIDDEN TREASURE

I got in the bath,
Most very last,
I took out the plug and got sucked down the drain,
I went so fast, like a speeding train.

It was like another world,
Just waiting to be explored.

I could feel something behind me,
I turned around.
'Ah, a shark!' in the dark.
I swam on, I saw a chest.
I opened it, then
'Robert, get out of the bath *now*!' said my mum.

The next day I got back in,
There it was.
I opened it.
There's rubies, pearls, silver gold
And a shiny diamond,
Huge it was.

I touched it, I started to glow and glow
And then I woke up in time for *school!*

Lewis Andrews (10)
St Ignatius RC Primary School, Sunbury-on-Thames

FBI

'Quick, put it in a box.'
'You look out for Uncle Knox.'
In came Uncle Knox looking quite cross.
He asked me if I'd seen a multicoloured box.
He went downstairs
And phoned the FBI.
I began to cry.
They took up all the floorboards.
They found the hidden sweets.
I really thought I was going to die.
I really was quite dumb
But deep in the refrigerator
The hidden treasure lies.
No one to disturb it,
Not even I.

Daniel Olguin (9)
St Ignatius RC Primary School, Sunbury-on-Thames

WHAT IS BLUE?

Rivers are blue
Seas are blue
Blue is new
Chelsea are blue

The chairs are blue
Blue is shiny
Blue is St John Fisher
Paper boxes are blue

Blue is neat like heat.

Oscar Finn (8)
St Ignatius RC Primary School, Sunbury-on-Thames

HEART OF MEMORY

He's gone, disappeared
For ever more
My closest friend
And his name was Tibor.

With a silky mane
That swung in the breeze
His favourite place was
The hill with the trees.

He won 15 races
For jumping high and low
He loved it when the man said,
'Ready, set, go.'

The accident happened
As we were riding to the show
A car came whizzing by
And skidded on the snow.

It knocked Tibor down
And the vets came by
They told me he was dead
And I started to cry.

He's gone for ever more
As you can see
Even though he's dead
He's in my *heart of memory.*

Emily Harrison (9)
St Ignatius RC Primary School, Sunbury-on-Thames

TEN LITTLE PETS

Ten little pets wanted their food so they pined
One ran away and then there were *nine.*

Nine little pets running to the gate
One crashed and then there were *eight.*

Eight little pets off to Woolworths for a pick 'n' mix
One preferred chocolate and then there were *six.*

Six little pets looking in a hive
Along came a bear and then there were *five.*

Five little pets cleaning their paws
One didn't clean it and then there were *four.*

Four little pets kissing in a tree
One skipped off then there were *three.*

Three little pets lived in the zoo
One went for a chat and then there were *two.*

Two little pets looking for a bone, thought there was none
But they found it and then there was *one.*

One little pet had a toy hero
But she couldn't find it and then there was *zero.*

Sarah Kane (7)
St Ignatius RC Primary School, Sunbury-on-Thames

TWINKLE, TWINKLE LITTLE BAT

Twinkle, twinkle little bat
How I wonder what you splat
Like a toilet in the sky
Goes down the sewer like a fly

Flitter, flutter here and there
He always sleeps under the chair
He may be silly, he may be rude
The problem is he eats too much food.

Ciara Reed (9)
St Ignatius RC Primary School, Sunbury-on-Thames

RUNAWAY HAMSTER

I have a hidden treasure
His fur was white as snow
Everyone knows

Just lately I saw him crawling
Among the hay and dung
But now he's out exploring
Among the old and young

I tried him on his pager
He would not return my call
But I think he's in South America
Swimming in a pool

Or maybe he's filling his tummy
On things hamsters like best
Or on a beach in Las Vegas
Wearing the top velvet vest!

But I think he's back; yes, I'm sure
Maybe I'll look just once more
Yes, he's back and I am sure about that
He's my hidden treasure!

Naomi Buck (10)
St Ignatius RC Primary School, Sunbury-on-Thames

TEN LITTLE CHILDREN

Ten little children drinking wine,
One got drunk and then there were *nine.*

Nine little children standing with a mate,
One started gossiping and then there were *eight.*

Eight little children going to Devon,
One fell off the train and then there were *seven.*

Seven little children making a mix,
One ate it all and then there were *six.*

Six little children walking past a hive,
One got stung and then there were *five.*

Five little children begging for more,
One said, 'Please' and then there were *four.*

Four little children climbing up a tree,
One fell down and then there were *three.*

Three little children trying to fit in a show,
One popped out and then there were *two.*

Two little children playing in the sun,
One got hot and then there was *one.*

One little child trying to a hero,
He got scared and then there were *zero.*

Ellie Hill (7)
St Ignatius RC Primary School, Sunbury-on-Thames

TEN LITTLE CHILDREN

Ten little children feeling rather fine,
One got sick and then there were *nine*.

Nine little children came to school late,
One got detention and then there were *eight*.

Eight little children going up to Heaven,
One got lost and then there were *seven*.

Seven little children doing magic tricks,
One got zapped and then there were *six*.

Six little children playing near a hive,
Along came a bee and then there were *five*.

Five little children exploring a moor,
One fell in a bog and then there were *four*.

Four little children climbing up a tree,
One fell down and then there were *three*.

Three little children visiting London Zoo,
The lion ate one of them and then there were *two*.

Two little children playing with a gun,
One got shot and then there was *one*.

One little child eating a bun,
He choked on a currant and then there were none.

George Standbridge (8)
St Ignatius RC Primary School, Sunbury-on-Thames

TEN LITTLE CHILDREN

Ten little children all drinking wine,
One got drunk and then there were *nine*.

Nine little children eating a cake,
One fell ill and then there were *eight*.

Eight little children went to Devon,
One got lost and then there were *seven*.

Seven little children all playing with bricks,
One cracked his head and then there were *six*.

Six little children all went for a drive,
One got run over and then there were *five*.

Five little children having a war,
One got shot and then there were *four*.

Four little children climbing a tree,
One fell down and then there were *three*.

Three little children with nothing to do,
One fell asleep and then there were *two*.

Two little children laying in the sun,
One got burnt and then there was *one*.

One little child cried for his mum,
She came along and then there were *none*.

Amy Plummer (8)
St Ignatius RC Primary School, Sunbury-on-Thames

TEN LITTLE CHILDREN

Ten little children standing in a line,
One fell down the stairs and then there were *nine.*

Nine little children sitting at the gate,
One ran away and then there were *eight.*

Eight little children travelling to Devon,
One stayed back and then there were *seven.*

Seven little children playing with sticks,
One got hurt and then there were *six.*

Six little children waiting to dive,
One tripped over and then there were *five.*

Five little children playing with a saw,
One hurt his finger and then there were *four.*

Four little children saw a bee,
One got stung and then there were *three.*

Three little children playing in the dew,
One fell over and then there were *two.*

Two little children eating a bun,
One got poisoned and then there was *one.*

One little child having fun,
He went home and then there were *none!*

Michael Francis-Lynch (7)
St Ignatius RC Primary School, Sunbury-on-Thames

TEN LITTLE CHILDREN

Ten little children feeling so fine,
Along came a dog and then there were *nine*.

Nine little children at the school fete,
One got knocked out and then there were *eight*.

Eight little children trying to get to Heaven,
Along came an angel and then there were *seven*.

Seven little children eating pic 'n' mix,
One ate too much and then there were *six*.

Six little children having a dive,
One hit his head and then there were *five*.

Five little children opening a door,
One got hit and then there were *four*.

Four little children sitting on a tree,
One went to sleep and then there were *three*.

Three little children dancing in the glue,
One got stuck and then there were *two*.

Two little children eating a bun,
One didn't like it and then there was *one*.

One little child having fun,
He tripped up and then there were *none*.

Jordan Delaney (8)
St Ignatius RC Primary School, Sunbury-on-Thames

TEN LITTLE CHILDREN

Ten little children drinking wine,
One got drunk and then there were *nine*.

Nine little children smashing plates,
One ran off and then there were *eight*.

Eight little children playing in Heaven ,
One fell down and then there were *seven*.

Seven little children piling bricks
They all fell and then there were *six*.

Six little children going to dive,
One fell in and then there *five*.

Five little children jumping on the floor,
One fell through and then there were *four*.

Four little children swimming in the sea,
Along came a shark and then there were *three*.

Three little children making stew,
One got burnt and then there were *two*.

Two little children having fun
One got hurt and then there was *one*.

One little child bored and glum.
He went off then there were *none*.

Joseph White (8)
St Ignatius RC Primary School, Sunbury-on-Thames

TEN LITTLE CHILDREN

Ten little children watching a pantomime,
One got scared by the beast and then there were *nine*.

Nine little children got to school late,
One went to the Headmaster and then there were *eight*.

Eight little children going to see Devon,
One stayed for tea and then there were *seven*.

Seven little children counting statistics,
One got muddled up and then there were *six*.

Six little children looking at a hive,
One got stung and that left *five*.

Five little children trying to ignore,
One walked away and that left *four*.

Four little children swimming hopelessly,
One got eaten by a shark and then there were *three*.

Three little children sticking things with glue,
One got stuck to the page and then there were *two*.

Two little children lived in Shepperton,
One moved to Sunbury and that left *one*.

One little child shouted, *'Kzung,'*
She magically disappeared and that left *none*.

Alexandra Alderson (8)
St Ignatius RC Primary School, Sunbury-on-Thames

TEN LITTLE CHILDREN

Ten little children drinking wine,
One got drunk and then there were *nine.*

Nine little children eating grapes,
One got sick and then there were *eight.*

Eight little children standing by a gate,
One went to live in Devon and then there were *seven.*

Seven little children stepping on stones,
One picked up sticks and then there were *six.*

Six little children picking up sticks,
One found a beehive and then there were *five.*

Five little children run from the beehive,
One went indoors and then there were *four.*

Four little children playing around a tree,
One hurt his knee and then there were *three.*

Three little children standing in the cold,
One felt blue and then there were *two.*

Two little children doing up their shoes,
One fell on his bum and then there was *one.*

One little child was trying to be a hero,
He got afraid and then there were *zero.*

Rebecca Raymond (8)
St Ignatius RC Primary School, Sunbury-on-Thames

TEN LITTLE CHILDREN

Ten little children feeling their spine,
One had to go to the doctor and then there were *nine*.

Nine little children choosing their mate,
One got thrown out and then there were *eight*.

Eight little children who are eleven,
One turned twelve and then there were *seven*.

Seven little children picking up sticks,
One cut his knee and then there were *six*.

Six little children singing to a hive,
One lost their voice and then there were *five*.

Five little children buying a saw,
One cut his head off and then there were *four*.

Four little children looking at a bee,
One got stung and then there were *three*.

Three little children needing the loo,
One went and then there were *two*.

Two little children waiting to see John,
One was sick and then there was *one*.

One little child eating a bun,
She was sick and then there were *none*.

Catherine Taylor (8)
St Ignatius RC Primary School, Sunbury-on-Thames

TEN LITTLE CHILDREN

Ten little children looking at the sunshine,
One became blind and then there were *nine*.

Nine little children waiting to ice-skate,
One slipped over and then there were *eight*.

Eight little children travelling to Heaven,
One was very naughty and then there were *seven*.

Seven little children learning how to fix,
One lost his tools and then there were *six*.

Six little children learning how to drive,
One nearly crashed and then there were *five*.

Five little children going on a tour,
One got lost and then there were *four*.

Four little children round the Christmas tree,
One went to church and then there were *three*.

Three little children swam the ocean blue,
One nearly drowned and then there were *two*.

Two little children sharing a hot cross bun,
One ran away and then there was *one*.

One little child looking hard for Ben,
He found the others and then there were *ten* again!.

Ryan Jardine (7)
St Ignatius RC Primary School, Sunbury-on-Thames

TEN LITTLE CHILDREN

Ten little children waiting to dine,
One got fed up and then there were *nine*.

Nine little children waiting by a gate,
One walked through and then there were *eight*.

Eight little children sitting in their den,
One went home and then there were *seven*.

Seven little children picking up sticks,
One got lost and then there were *six*.

Six little children visiting a hive,
One got stung and then there were *five*.

Five little children sitting on the floor,
One got up and then there were *four*.

Four little children standing under a tree,
One climbed up and then there were *three*.

Three little children at the zoo,
One got lost and then there were *two*.

Two little children playing and having fun,
One went on the swing and then there was *one*.

One little child swinging in the sun,
His mother took home so then there were *zero*.

Dale Moore-Saxton (7)
St Ignatius RC Primary School, Sunbury-on-Thames

TEN LITTLE CHILDREN

Ten little children studying in school,
One felt sick, the others felt cool.

Nine little children, some had a mate,
One didn't have any so left the school and then there were *eight*.

Eight little children looking for Heaven,
One went back and then there were *seven*.

Seven little children picked up the sticks,
Along came a tiger and then there were *six*.

Six little children went to see the hive,
The bee stung one of them and then there were *five*.

Five little children banging on the door,
One was caught by the police and then there were *four*.

Four little children climbing up a tree,
One fell down and broke his leg and then there were *three*.

Three little children were Rebecca me and you,
Rebecca went home now there are *two*.

Two little children baking a bun,
One burnt his hand and then there was *one*.

One little child proved he was a hero,
He also left the classroom and then there was *zero*.

Ria Pereira (7)
St Ignatius RC Primary School, Sunbury-on-Thames

TEN LITTLE CHILDREN

Ten little children waiting to get a fine,
One jumped out of the window and then there were *nine*.

Nine little children all ready to inflate,
One went *pop!* and then there were *eight*.

Eight little children waiting to go to Heaven,
One got up there and then there were *seven*.

Seven little children playing just for kicks,
One forgot to tie his lace and then there were *six*.

Six little children waiting to see Clive,
One got knocked out and then there were *five*.

Five little children on a wild boar,
One fell off and then there were *four*.

Four little children dancing with glee,
One fell over and then there were *three*.

Three little children standing in a queue,
One decided not to wait and then there were *two*.

Two little children sticking out their tongues,
One got sent home and that left *one*.

One little child having fun,
He disappeared in a cloud of smoke and then there were *none*.

Thomas Smallbone (8)
St Ignatius RC Primary School, Sunbury-on-Thames

TEN LITTLE CHILDREN

Ten little children drinking wine,
One got drunk and then there were *nine.*

Nine little children going on a date,
Along came a lion and then there were *eight.*

Eight little children trying to get to Heaven,
Along came an angel and then there were *seven.*

Seven little children playing with sticks,
Along came the teacher and then there were *six.*

Six little children trying to drive,
Along came a bomb and then there were *five.*

Five little children were very, very poor,
One died and then there were *four.*

Four little children sitting by a tree,
The tree fell down and then there were *three.*

Three little children sitting on the loo,
Then one flushed it and then there were *two.*

Two little children going for a run,
One tripped up and then there was *one.*

One little child eating a plum,
He choked on the stone and then there were *none.*

Rebecca Kirby (7)
St Ignatius RC Primary School, Sunbury-on-Thames

TEN LITTLE CHILDREN

Ten little children standing in a line,
One ran away and then there were *nine*.

Nine little children swinging on a gate,
One fell off and then there were *eight*.

Eight little children living in Devon,
One moved away and then there were *seven*.

Seven little children doing some tricks,
One disappeared and then there were *six*.

Six little children found a beehive,
One got stung and then there were *five*.

Five little children found a secret door,
One went through it and then there were *four*.

Four little children hurt their knees,
One went to hospital and then there were *three*.

Three little children paddling in a canoe,
One fell in and then there were *two*.

Two little children having lots of fun,
One fell asleep and then there was *one*.

One little child sitting in the sun,
Mum called her in and then there were *none*.

Imogen Buck (7)
St Ignatius RC Primary School, Sunbury-on-Thames

TEN LITTLE CHILDREN

Ten little children doing just fine,
Along came a gust of wind and then there were *nine*.

Nine little children trying not to be late,
One missed the bus and then there were *eight*.

Eight little children driving to Devon,
The wheel fell off and then there were *seven*.

Seven little children nicking pic 'n' mix,
Along came the manager and then there were *six*.

Six little children messing with a hive,
Along came a bee and then there were *five*.

Five little children playing with a door,
One got his finger trapped and then there were *four*.

Four little children eating their tea,
One got poisoned and then there were *three*.

Three little children going to Waterloo,
One got run over and then there were *two*.

Two little children eating an iced bun,
One ran home and then there was *one*.

One little child sitting in the sun,
He melted and then there were *none*.

William Daly (7)
St Ignatius RC Primary School, Sunbury-on-Thames

TEN LITTLE CHILDREN

Ten little children drinking wine,
One got sick and then there were *nine*.

Nine little children kissing their mate,
One tripped up and then there were *eight*.

Eight little children going to Devon,
One when to Heaven and then there were *seven*.

Seven little children making a mix,
One go till and then there were *six*.

Six little children standing by a hive,
One got sung and then there were *five*.

Five little children sitting on the floor,
One got hit and then there were *four*.

Four little children full of glee,
One got sad and then there were *three*.

Three little children waiting for stew,
One went to the loo and then there were *two*.

Two little children eating a bun,
One sank in and then there was *one*.

One little child standing in the sun,
She got burnt and then there were *none*.

Vivien Miller (8)
St Ignatius RC Primary School, Sunbury-on-Thames

BENEATH THE SEA

Beneath the sea
Is a hidden treasure
It is in the wreck of a ship

Beneath the sea
In the cabin of the ship
That lay there on its own

Beneath the sea
Somewhere along the seabed
The key to open the box

Beneath the sea
The box to the treasure
Yes, that's it

Beneath the sea
I've found it
That place

Beneath the sea
Open the door and . . .
I've found the treasure

It's in a big box
With crowns, jewels and . . .

Wow, well . . .
I don't know what to say
Everything you can think of
It's in that box.

Kathryn Tyler (10)
St Ignatius RC Primary School, Sunbury-on-Thames

SECRET PHOTOS

I have a secret
No one else knows about,
It's very special to me
Without a doubt.

Under the loose floorboard
In my room,
Are my secret photos
Of a bride and groom.

There's my grandad
Nice and smart,
Thinks he's young
Got an important part.

Yes, you've guessed it
It's my mum and dad,
That they got married
I'm so glad.

They invited lots
Of people there,
They are such
A happy pair.

So now you know
The secret in my room,
My secret photos
Of a bride and groom.

Kate England (10)
St Ignatius RC Primary School, Sunbury-on-Thames

THE BOARD RUBBER

My name is Jake
I love to eat cake
But I cannot take
Not eating cake
Because I have to
Rake the leaves
I go to school
And I learn all
Day and when
The day is down
I go to see my
Mum but then I
Remembered
I left my bag
So back I go
Into school
To find my bag
So then as I'm
Walking out, bag in hand
Tap, tap, tap rubber on the blackboard
Open swings the blackboard, silver and gold
In I go
Bang swings the blackboard
There's me covered in silver and gold
Yes, all mine
I'm rich, I'm rich
Lots of cake for me.

Edward Finn (10)
St Ignatius RC Primary School, Sunbury-on-Thames

MY LITTLE BROTHER

My little brother
Is like no other
And that you can't deny
He laughs and plays
In his mischievous ways
And keeps coming for more
His bouncing balls
Hit the walls
He loves looking at ants
And it tickles
When he gets them
In his pants.
So I say
Look out
When my little brother
Is about!

Olivia Flowerday (8)
St Ignatius RC Primary School, Sunbury-on-Thames

WHAT IS GREEN?

The green grass
Rushes past
When you travel
Fast.

The green Irish shamrock is
Bright green
But if it jumps out
In front of you
You may scream.

Green can be your favourite colour
But when you receive
Your green, woolly jumper from your
Aunt Mabel
Green may not be your favourite.

Camilla Smallbone (9)
St Ignatius RC Primary School, Sunbury-on-Thames

ANOTHER DIMENSION

I have a hidden treasure
That no one even knows
A plain wall I thought
Then a door shape grows.

I walked through
I saw another dimension
It looked brand new
It suddenly caught my attention.

I spent the whole day there
I didn't have a care
I met some new friends
I gave my friends a dare.

It's time for me to go
And for me to say goodbye
To leave this world behind
Oh, time does fly by!

Suzanne Marie O'Beirne (9)
St Ignatius RC Primary School, Sunbury-on-Thames

BIRDS, BEES AND SEAS

The birds, bees and seas are all part of the world.
The grass is their oyster and the puddles their pearls.

All animals, birds and reptiles share this world with us,
But what we use the world for, causes such a fuss.
We pollute its once fresh air, causing such despair,
And not only do we cut its trees . . . we also kill all birds and bees!

The birds, bees and seas are all part of this world.
The trees are their oyster and the puddles their pearls.

The birds, bees and seas are all part of this world.
The trees are their oyster and the puddles their pearls.

Without its natural resources and running rivers too
We would be without medication, to recover us from flu.
Cars and jumpers, T-shirts and many things besides,
Are all things that come from the ground, things that nature provides.

The birds, bees and seas are all part of this world.
The grass is their oyster and the puddles their pearls.

The birds, bees and seas are all part of this world.
The grass is their oyster and the puddles their pearls.

If we keep doing these things that cause such a fuss
We will no longer be living on this Earth, plus . . .
To ruin this Earth would be a dreadful thing.
So why not help us? *Put your litter in the bin!*

Verity Rolfe (11)
St Ignatius RC Primary School, Sunbury-on-Thames

THE SHIP'S MAIDEN

When the fishermen have gone,
And noise and chatter are far,
She appears in her dirty rags,
Shining like the stars.

She's a ship's maiden,
From the old,
She is now dead,
She lost her life for gold.

No one knows her name,
Or her family,
But I wonder if her parents know
That she's a ghost maiden out at sea?

So when you are tucked up in bed tonight,
Cosy, comfy and yawning,
Listen carefully for the ghost maiden's cries,
Her soulful, sorrowful mourning.

Lauren Stone (10)
St Ignatius RC Primary School, Sunbury-on-Thames

KNIGHT

K   ind people sleep
N   ipping bugs creep
I   llegal pigs reek
G   alloping unicorns meet
H   ighly martial arts mice squeak
T   hreatening monsters make the heat.

PJ Walsh (8)
St Ignatius RC Primary School, Sunbury-on-Thames

FIREWORKS

I like fireworks
Because they're nice
Like a picture in the sky
With glitter everywhere.

I like to see and stare
I like to see them in the parks
Shining up everywhere.

Sometimes I hear them bang
So I look out of the window with a fright
Thinking something happened
But then I saw a beautiful fireworks in the sky
And then I laughed.

Ana Gouvéia (10)
St Ignatius RC Primary School, Sunbury-on-Thames

THE STREET

People rushing, pushing, shoving on their busy lives
Children running, playing games

And then it's me playing at the stall all alone
Market stalls selling

And then it's me playing at the stall all alone
I get caught in the rush
I find myself on the deck
To my amazement this boy helps me up
Cars racing

And then it's me playing with my friend.

Peter Ward (9)
St Ignatius RC Primary School, Sunbury-on-Thames

What Is Yellow?

Yellow is the sun in the sky
Yellow is the sunflower saying hello
Yellow is an arrow pointing north
Pop stars wearing yellow and singing
Yellow is a good colour in the morning
Jesus comes with the colour
Yellow is a hair band that a girl wears
Yellow is a power ranger fighting crime
Yellow is a butterfly born
Yellow is sand on the beach
Yellow is honey that bears eat
Yellow is a desert
Yellow is the moon shining
Yellow is for more.

Claurina Movakhomo (9)
St Ignatius RC Primary School, Sunbury-on-Thames

Hidden Treasure

In a dark, dark street,
In a dark, dark house,
Under a dark, dark bed.
There was a dark, dark box,
And in the dark, dark box,
There was a dark, dark alley,
And in the dark, dark alley,
There was a dark, dark room,
And in the dark, dark room,
There was a golden case,
And in the golden case,
There was *hidden treasure.*

Sean Hill (10)
St Ignatius RC Primary School, Sunbury-on-Thames

THE BOX

There was a box in the attic,
I looked in it.
It was full of beautiful treasures,
Kept from the past.
There was a locket.
I opened it.
It was a photo of Sunset,
My hamster.
My dear Sunset,
My sweet Sunset.

I took the box to my room,
The very next day.
I looked in the box again.
It was a dusty, old book.
It had poems about
My hamsters,
My dear hamsters,
My sweet hamsters.
It was a treasure kept
From the past.

Elizabeth Wilson (10)
St Ignatius RC Primary School, Sunbury-on-Thames

UNTITLED

I will play in my box
I will invite everyone for dinner
Then we can go and play
In my box, of course.

Alma Kalaji (10)
Springfield Primary School

THE MAGIC BOX

I will put in my box
A black rug that looks like mud,
A horse with bright green eyes and white fur,
A heart that's been pulled out of an Egyptian body.

I will put in my box
Something special to me,
My pet because it is noisy at night,
I will put my dummies from when I was born.

I will put in my box
A photo of my family,
I will put my glass ornaments in,
My stereo player in to make it better.

I will put in my box
A tub full of chocolates,
A horn of a deer,
My food that I buy.

My box is made of
Iron and wood plus metal,
With shiny, brass hinges,
It has Egyptians staring at you.

I will go to the seaside with my dad,
I will go and climb the mountain in Scotland,
I will go to the Dudley's house and see Harry Potter,
I will go to Egypt.

Kelly Rogers (9)
Springfield Primary School

DAYDREAMS

Mrs Hastings thinks I'm reading
But no
I'm on holiday relaxing on a hot breach with a light breeze.
I'm having good time with my friends.
I'm flying high in the air with joy.
I'm diving in the cool breeze sea.
I'm a happy millionaire.
I'm flying around the world.
I'm talking to animals.

Mrs Hastings thinks I'm listening
But no
I'm the strongest man in the world who could lift anything.
I'm slaying vampires with Buffy.
I'm driving the fastest sports car in the world with the wind blowing
in my face.
I'm the best James Bond.
I'm the best in the world
But I'm suddenly woken by the moaning of my friend Andrew.

Nixon Tsan (11)
Springfield Primary School

DAYDREAMS

Mrs Hastings thinks I'm reading
But no
I'm on the moon with my dog
I'm swimming through vibrant corals
I'm running on a sandy beach
I'm floating on a big cloud
I'm on a white horse riding through the dark wood
I'm going out shopping with only £10.

Mrs Hastings thinks I'm listening
But no
I have just done my SATs and I am on my way to Devon
I'm riding on a tiger hunting its prey
I'm flying over the sea
I'm running to a world full of chocolate
Now all my daydreams are over from the sound of the fire bell.
'Ding, ding.'

Casey Arbery (11)
Springfield Primary School

DAYDREAMS

Mrs Hastings thinks I'm reading,
But no,
I'm away in California,
I'm riding on beautiful horses,
I'm swimming with dolphins in the tropical sea,
I'm shopping my heart away,
I'm buying anything I want,
I'm having lunch with my mater,
I have four St Bernard dogs running freely
Making sure no one would hurt me,
I'm meeting Blue, they take me to a recording studio
And I get to sing a single with them,
I'm being rewarded by Blue, they've bought me a manor,
They've hired 100 servants for me so I have a couple for each job,
I'm having a room turned into a room for dogs so they are in
                                                    Heaven too
I have a letter in the post saying I have won £1,000 to spend on me,
Then my friend kicks me and says,
'Mrs Hastings is waiting for your answer.'

Emily Smith (11)
Springfield Primary School

DAYDREAMS

Mrs Hastings thinks I'm reading.
But no.
I'm the world's best dancer.
I'm dancing with Misteeq.
Now I'm in the sky.
I'm dancing with the stars in the midnight sky.
I'm flying like a bird.
I'm sleeping on a cloud.
I'm riding a white horse through the misty sky.

Mrs Hastings thinks I'm listening.
But no.
I'm playing football in the women's team.
I'm playing for England.
I'm racing a cheetah in the jungle.
I'm the world's fastest animal.
Suddenly the daydreams are over
By the music of Misteeq.

Chelsea Poulter (10)
Springfield Primary School

DAYDREAMS

Mrs Hastings thinks I'm reading.
But no.
I'm riding the streets in my ice cream car
And feeling a little peckish,
I'm diving and communicating with dolphins in Florida,
I'm having the most amazing sleepover
With all of my friends and my favourite band turn up,
I'm flying in the air listening to private conversations,
I'm making my great nanny get better.

Mrs Hastings thinks I'm listening.
But no.
I'm being a pop star,
Being famous and getting wealthier,
I'm the owner of a million horses,
I've passed my SATs and GCSEs and got a good grade.

'You can go out to lunch now, Rachel.'

Rachel Barnes (11)
Springfield Primary School

DAYDREAMS

Mrs Hastings thinks I'm reading
But no
I'm getting chased by a great white shark
I'm now getting flashed away to Germany to see a football match
I'm now on the pitch scoring the winning goal

Mrs Hastings thinks I'm listening
But no
I'm riding on a lion's back, no I'm not
I'm inside the PlayStation 2 actually
I'm driving a red sports car now
I'm riding on a flying horse

Mrs Hastings thinks I'm writing
But no
I'm swimming with dolphins, no I'm not
I'm winning a million pounds actually
Mrs Hastings is asking me a question.

Matthew Percy (10)
Springfield Primary School

DAYDREAMS

Mrs Hastings thinks I'm reading,
But I'm not,
I'm swimming with gorgeous, shiny dolphins in the deep blue sea,
I'm getting my bedroom ready for a girl's night in,
I'm on my way to a Chelsea football match,
I'm going on a shopping spree with only £50,
I'm sunbathing in sunny Lanzarote,
I'm in my pyjamas watching a soppy, love film,
I'm laying on my bed listening to music,
I'm winning a race on sports day,
I'm eating yummy chocolate!

Mrs Hastings thinks I'm listening,
But no,
I'm snorkelling at the bottom of the sea,
My leg is getting caught in the beautiful coral,
I'm speaking to animals,
I'm riding my handsome, white horse,
Galloping through the long grass on a summer's day,
I've completed my SATs and we're on our way to Devon,
I've just started Thamesmead and made loads of friends already,
I'm going with my whole family to Florida,
I'm in the middle of our class assembly and my mind has gone blank,
It is lunchtime!

'You can go out to lunch now, Ellie.'
Great, it's now lunchtime, I've done no work at all. (Oh dear).

Ellie-May Lockyer (10)
Springfield Primary School

DAYDREAMS

Mrs Hastings thinks I'm reading,
But no.
I'm the very first person in space having a fight with an alien,
I'm riding an elephant in an African jungle,
I'm swinging on all the trees with my monkey friends,
I'm being chased by a great white shark in the deepest depths
of the ocean

Mrs Hastings thinks I'm listening,
But no.
I'm watching my favourite TV show,
I'm saving the world from an alien invasion,
I'm flying with the birds in the sky,
I'm standing on top of the world,
I'm jumping off a tip of a cliff and ending up without a scratch.

Mrs Hastings thinks I'm working,
But no.
I'm surfing down a rocky waterfall,
I'm flying without wings,
I'm climbing a mountain in a day,
I'm riding on a dolphin's back as we whizz through the enchanted
sea doing tricks

I hear Mrs Hastings calling me.
I must leave my dream world behind.

Alix Scott (11)
Springfield Primary School

THE MAGIC BOX

I will put in my box
A shark with big rings in his ears.
A crocodile next to a rat.
A cowboy with sword and dagger.

I will put in my box
A deep sea diver wearing Sunday best.
A witch with a stick and a dog with a wand.
A knight with a shotgun and pistol.

I will put in my box
A king with a sword in his head and a nerd with a crown on his head.
A sun that will stay in the same place.
A pen that will write on its own.

I will put in my box
A fish in a box, a pair of shoes in a fish tank.
A saw that would cut on its own.
An oven that would cook four dinners at once.

I had made my box like
The queen's jewellery box.
The hinges are made out of ducks beak
Every corner is filled with gold.

I shall swim in the tropical sea.
I will ride on a shark's back.
I will walk a marathon.
I shall climb Mount Everest.

Paul Filbey (9)
Springfield Primary School

THE MAGIC BOX

I will put in my box
Millions of small, purple rubies,
A coin carved with my name on,
A shiny star as tiny as an ant.

I will put in my box
My teddy bear that I had when I was a baby
And my ring on it.

I will put in my box
A shining silver diamond
The diamond was so shiny it made my eyes twinkle,
And a picture of me when I was a pop star
When I was a baby.

I will put in my box
A big, shiny model that I made
When I was in play school when I was a baby,
A medal that my dad got me on my first birthday.

The hinges of my box are made out of sharks' teeth,
The shape of my box is a circle,
It has Chinese pictures on it.

A starfish shining in the sky,
Blue with all their albums,
A fish that talks,
A zombie that comes out at day.

Jade Dunning (10)
Springfield Primary School

THE MAGIC BOX

I will put in my box
A crystal clear dolphin
A magic key that opens anything
A knight on a Hoover.

I will put in my box
A bright sun so it wouldn't be dark
A watch that would stop time
A rubber that would rub ink.

I will put in my box
A web that is made out of silver
A big chocolate so when you eat it, it comes back
A hat, where you wish it comes true.

I will put in my box
A witch on a camel
A king on a broomstick
A shark tooth that is clear gold.

My box is made from crystal and ice
With hearts and glitters on top of the lid
A star on each little corner
A heart shape right in the middle.

I shall ride on a flying pig in my magic box
So I could go to places where I haven't been
And eat as many sweets as I like.

Emma Ly (10)
Springfield Primary School

THE MAGIC BOX

I will put in my box
The powder of an old potion
A gold ring glowing in the dark
The fire blazing in a pit.

I will put in my box
A smoking pig with a pie
The noise of a squirrel opening his nut
And the witch on a vacuum cleaner.

I will put in my box
A boom from a cannon
A pot full of money
And the teacher's in a corner.

I will put in my box
A dragon as yellow as the sun
The wave of a magic key
And the colour of the morning sun rising.

My box is built from steel
A picture of a musician on the sides
And the stars which twinkle in the night
The moon on the top of the box lights up the night sky.

I shall count my shiny money
And read some fairly tall books at night
And eat chocolate until I am sick.

Michael Thompson (10)
Springfield Primary School

THE MAGIC BOX

I will put in my box
The galaxy locked in a diamond,
The head of a gorgon,
Black fire that came from nowhere.

I will put in my box
The blinding light of the sun,
A key that opens a door to the next dimension,
A one pence coin that could buy you anything.

I will put in my box
A crystal clear eagle,
A statue of me made from pennies,
The world made of fruit pastilles.

I will put in my box
A ring that can summon evil spirits,
A man with his arms and legs swapped round,
A book made of paper clips.

My box is created with water and fire,
A lock that disappears,
Planets and moons on the lid,
And a rainbow in the middle.

I shall party in my box
On an island far away,
Then fall into the comfiest bed,
And watch myself fall asleep.

Royston Poplett (10)
Springfield Primary School

My Magic Box

I will put in my box
The slow movement of a large snail
An Egyptian pyramid made from sand
Steam from the boiling nostrils of a green dragon
The growl of a fierce tiger.

I will put in my box
Santa Claus and his little helpers
Ten gallons of water from an ancient lake
A strand of hair from a newborn baby.

I will put in my box
A pineapple picked from an apple tree
A picture of my future
The rounded hat worn by a Mexican
The first planet ever discovered.

I will put in my box
Seven bars of gleaming gold
A clock which never tells the proper time
A black cat that is lucky
The newly-grown teeth of a ten-year-old.

My box is styled with sticks and leaves
It is a tree shape
The inside is covered with green silk
Its hinges are made from stones.

I will walk around the world in my box
I shall collect souvenirs from different places
Then I shall zoom back home in a rocket.

Jodie Spragg (9)
Springfield Primary School

THE MAGIC BOX

I will put in the box
The first tooth of a baby
A brick from the Queen's palace
One of Henry VIII's engagement rings.

I will put in the box
A cheeky smile of a Chinese cheetah
The first glow of a star
The first leaf on a tree.

I will put in the box
A claw from a dinosaur
A magic spell cast by a witch
The first ever animal that roamed on Earth.

I will put in the box
A solid gold tooth
A hair plucked from an elephant's tail
The first written word from a man.

My box is fashioned with tinsel and fire
It is as round as the run
It is crammed with objects from top to bottom
It has a lock that only a magic key can open.

I shall sunbathe in my box
On a yellow beach washed up by the sea
Under the bright sun
In Spain.

Hannah Lee (10)
Springfield Primary School

MAGIC BOX

I will put in my box
A silver diamond from a golden ring,
Feathers from the softest pillow,
A snowman from the white snow.

I will put in my box
A carving of me in England,
Fireworks from the midnight sky,
Bangers from the year 2002.

I shall put in my box
An ice cube as cold as a freezer,
A picture from a stained glass window,
A heart from a human body.

I shall put in my box
A dog from the world's greatest pet shop,
A shooting star as gold as ingots,
My name carved in wood.

My box is made from god, silver and bronze,
With gold bars for a lock,
Bronze stars on top,
And silver hinges.

I will ride in my box
A bike from England,
A camel from a desert,
A dragon from the heart of China.

Ben Carter (9)
Springfield Primary School

THE MAGIC BOX

I will put in my box
The Sphinx of ancient Egypt
A fossil from the dinosaur period
A blackbird biting the flesh of a worm.

I will put in my box
The last howl of a wolf
The last of Santa's elves
A coin that could buy you anything.

I will put in my box
The heart of a deer
The blinding light of the sun
The first planet of the solar system.

I will put in my box
A merman from the bottom of the sea
The pearl from an oyster
A clock that talks to you.

My box is styled with gold and silver
It is a pyramid
There are stars and moons inside the lid
The hinges are dinosaurs' feet.

I will ski in my box
And meet new friends
I will watch the best sunset
The colour of a flaming fire.

Katie-Anne McCarthy (10)
Springfield Primary School

THE MAGIC BOX

I will put in my box
A shark's sharpest tooth,
An Egyptian mummy,
The eye of an owl.

I will put in my box
A five-year holiday,
The wing of Pegasus,
The blood of Jesus.

I will put in my box
A shooting star,
The hoof of Taurus,
A tail of a dragon.

I will put in my box
Hades' head,
A pig with wings,
An alien's spaceship.

I will put in my box
All evil spirits,
A headless horseman,
A zombie.

My box is created out of a head of a bull,
With gold and silver on the lid,
And the hinges snakeskin.

I shall ride flying pigs in my box
To visit planets which aren't there,
And eat tons of sweets.

Joshua Albright (9)
Springfield Primary School

MY MAGIC BOX

I will put in my box
A 100 carat gold statue,
And a marble ring,
An emerald green egg.

I will put in my box
A jewel on fire,
An idiot doing mathematics,
And a bird flying without wings.

I will put in my box
A clown gliding through stars,
A cage made of fur,
And a cloud sinking in the sky.

I will put in my box
A PlayStation that doesn't play,
A sun that doesn't shine,
And a waterfall made of fire.

My box is made from cloud, platinum and moon cheese,
With every type of jewel saying my name,
Memories drifting along the bottom,
Its hinges are made of aqua blue tidal waves.

I will play football in my box
With no referee
And I shall be invincible
Compared to Stanley Matthews.

Christopher Modak (9)
Springfield Primary School

THE MAGIC BOX

In my box I will put
The swish feel of a silk curtain
I shall put in the first story told
A starlit sky which stuns the people of the lands.

In my box I will put
A ruby as red as a red, red rose
And a diamond as clear as the future
As well as my greatest memories.

In my box I will put
The best Christmas I've ever had
The brilliant laughter from friends and family
And a grain of sand from Egypt's finest desert.

In my box I will put
A statue of me that no one can break
The blood of a Dracula
And a key of information found by me
That can save the world.

My box is made of glass
And has a lock that not even the strongest man could break
Although it's made of glass
You cannot see the things inside.

I shall go to America
And visit Disneyland
And swim in the calmest
And clearest sea.

Emma Bright (10)
Springfield Primary School

THE MAGIC BOX

I will put in the box
Some sand that glitters more than gold
A diamond from the emperor's crown
A whisker from a lion who was king of the jungle.

I will put in the box
A fresh flamingo's flower that has been on its head
Since it was born
A sloth that runs as fast as a cheetah.

I will put in the box
A found sovereign which is worth more than a dinosaur bone
The tail of a toothless great white shark
The body of the first ever living human.

I will put in the box
The hair of the so-called Medusa
The noise of dripping blood from a vampire's victim
The laugh of a newborn baby.

I will put in the box
The sway of a wooden boat surviving a deadly storm
A whole black stripe off a tiger's fur
The Armada still battling in the Spanish seas.

My box is created with puma's fur and shaved teeth
With five thousand keys but only one can open my magic box
With crabs' golden claws to keep my secrets locked away
My box is the shape of nothing, is it not?

I will not sell my box for money or anything
I will hide my box, even from the king and queen
For nothing will get past me to get the box
I shall have my Magic Box buried with me!

Luke Ebsworth (9)
Springfield Primary School

THE MAGIC BOX

I will put in my box
A sapphire that shines like the sun,
A ruby as red as a crab,
A tooth from a fearsome snake.

I will put in my box
The snap of an alligator,
An emerald as green as the scales of a crocodile,
A pearl as smooth as a lion's mane.

I will put in my box
The fire of Hades,
The thunder of Zeus,
And the icy breath of the Loch Ness Monster.

I will put in my box
The heart of Tutankhamun,
The flame of a phoenix,
The grace of a peacock.

My box is fashioned from the scales of the aqua dragon,
With moons on the lid and fangs in its three corners,
The shape of my box is a pyramid with a curse only I can beat,
It has a password only I know.

I shall train in my box
With a boa constrictor,
Then race a cheetah,
As fast as a motorbike.

Martin Norman (9)
Springfield Primary School

My Magic Box

I will put in my box
A coin with my name on
A million small, purple rubies
A shiny star as tiny as an ant.

I will put in my box
A million dogs as tiny as a mouse
A book with a million pages
A shiny pen with a ruby.

I will put in my box
A talking dog
A library with many detective books
My computer games.

I will put in my box
A Lithuanian food.

Rimvydas Samonis (9)
Springfield Primary School

My Grandma

My grandma is my hidden treasure,
She used to have a lot of pleasure.
She will always be in my heart,
But now I have fallen apart.
Life without her is not the same,
But sometimes you have to take the pain.

Daljeet Kaur Kauldhar (11)
Tudor Primary School

My Hidden Treasure

My hidden treasure
Is here and there,
My hidden treasure
Is everywhere.
She's the one.
She's my mum.
We love each other,
More than anyone.
My mum's the one,
That I always hug.
She's the one,
I'll always love.
So now you know
Who's my hidden treasure.
We give each other
Love and pleasure.

Joyti Bhatti (10)
Tudor Primary School

Humpty Dumpty Went To The Moon

Humpty Dumpty went to the moon,
Humpty Dumpty saw a baboon,
When he arrived there,
The moon had so much light,
And was too bright,
Then Humpty Dumpty said to the moon
'I am going home in the afternoon.'

Gurpreet Ahitan (8)
Tudor Primary School

THE HIDDEN TREASURE

There is hidden treasure, where can it be?
Is it in your underwear? Let's look and see.
Is it in the washing machine, cleaning off the muck
Or maybe it's in the pond, swimming with the ducks?
Can it be in the bathroom, using the loo?
My sister came out and I said, *'Boo!'*
It might be in the kitchen, cooking me some food to eat
I went inside, it was quite tidy and neat.
Well, where can it be?
I looked near the dog, there were so many fleas.
Is it underneath the weeds in the sea
Or is it on the bed, sleeping next to me?
Could it be buried or lying in a ditch?
I feel quite scared, I think I'm getting an itch.
Is it in the attic, all old and dusty?
I feel a little worried in case it gets rusty.
It might be in space, it might be in Mars.
Oh my goodness, that is very far.
It might be in the fridge, keeping cool.
Look, Fred, it might be there, you old fool.
Are you in my cupboard? Let's check.
I looked in there, oh my, it's a wreck.
Shall we check the sink?
Oh my goodness, it really stinks.
Where can it be?
Maybe it is in my cup of tea.
Maybe it's an invisible treasure I wonder.
So with pleasure I will ponder
And guess what I've found?
The hidden treasure is in my dressing gown.

Orkid Catherine Wildman (10)
Tudor Primary School

HIDDEN TREASURE

Deep, deep down under the skin is my hidden heart,
It's growing and growing, faster and faster,
I and them should never part,
I'll always be in each other's heart.
They're implanted in my secret treasure
Bringing me so much willing pleasure.
We travel around feeling the same, hiding the pain
And feeling no shame.
Nobody knows what's happening inside
Because there's so many lies that I've told.
When I walked along the beach
I think of the victor's preach.
Express your feelings loud and clear
Have no fear, you're reaching near
As you walk you reach closer and closer.
When you reach your hidden heart
Don't forget the special part
It's waiting there for someone that's committed to care for you
Your heart and that special part.
One day I'll find it and next to it I'll sit all day
And all night.
Down they come and we'll go on a midnight flight
Up to the starry sky
Up, up we'll fly.
We'll come back up another night
I'll catch a star to keep
And treasure for ever and ever.
Now I've found that golden key to my hidden treasure
I'm as happy as ever
Knowing the golden key is attached
To the flying bird's feather.

Nickeisha Louise Roberts (10)
Tudor Primary School

SEEKING TREASURE

The gates of Heaven opens
For the search of the Heaven treasure
Hidden treasure instead I see a feature
A treasure feature I see

As I come close
The gates of Heaven close
The hidden treasure is lost
The feature fades away

The light shining upon me
Shines as it fills me with pride
I look and stare
I stare and look

The thunder strikes
The lightning strikes
I see my treasure
I see my feature

I am gifted from God
As God sent me this pride
Oh God, I thank You
For my hidden treasure

Treasure, treasure, treasure
My feature.

Sail Premgy (9)
Tudor Primary School

HIDDEN TREASURE

Deep inside the dark blue sea,
Lay the treasure of gold.
The petals glowing in the darkness.
The fishes are singing like they're in love.

The gold is singing to the water.
The litter is hitting the heart of gold.
And the sharks are biting the ribbons.
And the whale is singing the whale's song.

Karan Rauli (8)
Tudor Primary School

HIDDEN TREASURE

Is it hidden under the deep blue sea?
Does it hide the golden key?
Can it see what's inside of me?
Is it in the hot tea?
Is it as small as a flea?
Does it buzz like a bee?
Can it find hidden part?
Does it have a loving heat?
Can it ride the golden cart?
Can it paint a picture of art?
Does it drive a sports car?
Does it like to run far?
Does it swim with the fish or ready to be served in a dish?
Is it a whale or a male?
Does it know how to sail?
Does it own its own book?
Does it wear a blue coat?
Can it sink?
Does it have the brain to think?
Will it bring me a turtle dove or maybe a bit of caring love?
Can it sing a thing?
Can it tell the time in a little mime?
Can it feel pain or suck sugar cane?
Tell me, tell me and let me be.

Cherise Usiade (8)
Tudor Primary School

HIDDEN TREASURE

'Walk the plank,' said Pirate Tim.
'But, Captain Tim, I cannot swim.'
'Then you must win the hidden treasure
Then give it to me with all your pleasure.
All the money should be shiny good,
All the treasure must be sold.
With all that money we will be rich
To fill our tummy.
We will measure,
All the treasure.
We will be rich with our parrots.
Then he will be eating carrots.
Then we will find the treasure for hours.
When we find the treasure it will be ours.
First we will find the map,
Then we will hide it under my cap.
When we are rich,
We will destroy our shop.
Then we will take out our guns,
We will make sure Silly doesn't take his buns.'

Khalid Noor Mohamed (11)
Tudor Primary School

TREASURE

Treasure, treasure, give some pleasure,
Take my jewellery and measure,
Make me beautiful,
Make me wonderful,
Make me shine,
Make me fine.

Treasure, treasure, give some pleasure,
Take my junk and give me treasure,
Make me my crown,
Don't make a frown,
Make my jewellery soft,
Don't put it in the loft.

Treasure, treasure, give some pleasure.

Harkamal Deol (8)
Tudor Primary School

HIDDEN TREASURE

Hidden treasure, hidden
I am finding the treasure
Do you know where the treasure is?
Do you know what it looks like?
Everybody does not know where the treasure is
No one even knows where it is
The money is so shiny and the colour is gold and silver
Read, read the book of finding treasure then you will find it
Everybody, look, I found it
And I like to say to you thank you everybody!
Some of them are silver and gold
And some of them are white and brown
Umbrella, umbrella there are you, my friend
I've been finding you all day
Now it's your turn
Remember next time if there's gold we better get it
Everybody, let's go and find treasure once again.

Marjan Nadem (8)
Tudor Primary School

TREASURE

H   idden treasure, hidden treasure
I   t's my pleasure
D   iamonds and rubies
D   iamonds and gold
E   ggs for breakfast
N   utritious to find the treasure fast.

T   elescope and a map needed on the way
R   escue people in the day
E   yes to discover
A   nd guns and swords to kill
S   ome of your enemies and some of yourselves
U   need ships to sail along the ocean to the island
R   ubies and gold we found, going back now
E   eeeee hoooo, we are the successful pirates, the winners.

Gwlfam Mirza Baig (11)
Tudor Primary School

HIDDEN TREASURE

There are lots of hidden treasures in the world
Some are hard, some are easy.
Lots of them are on an island.
Have you ever found a hidden treasure?
Some pirates hide diamonds in the beach.

Captain Hook said (Pahiraties)
If they found hidden maps
To lead the way.
To lead the way to their lives.
Nobody ever found hidden treasure in 2002.
If they did they are so lucky.

Once Captain Hook lost his eye patch
And someone found it and hid it.
So someone found it and they got so lucky.
So start looking in your garden
Or if you go to the beach to find some
Hidden treasure!

Henna Ahmad (10)
Tudor Primary School

OBJECT POEM

Turtles are green,
Blue whales are blue,
Goldfishes are gold,
Snakes are slimy,
Fishes are all different colours like rainbow.

Cheetahs are yellow with black spots,
Lions' manes are hairy,
Snails are slithery,
Monkeys are mad,
Tarantulas are hairy with eight legs.

Rhinos are grey with pointy horns,
Apples are very delectable for a picnic,
Banana skis are slippery if you step on it,
Forks are sharp,
Knives are sharp as a shark's teeth.

Sheep have fluffy fur,
Eggs have yellow yolks,
Horses are really fast for races,
Zebras have black and white stripes,
Clocks are tick-tocking every time.

Afzal Ali (8)
Tudor Primary School

HIDDEN TREASURE

Diamond blue hair,
Smooth as silk,
While she walks on the pier,
She was on her journey,
To find the hidden treasure.

As she walks she hears,
The diamond blue waves,
Roaring and surging,
They smoothly wave.

The hidden treasure,
Has a secret pleasure,
Buried on another land,
She had broken her hand,
She plays for a band.

She silently waves bye
In her heart,
Dancing in glee by herself,
Her eyes sparkle brighter
Than a star.

The hidden treasure,
Has a secret measure,
She runs fast,
She's seen the treasure,
She opens it with pleasure.

Out pops a frog with a frown,
He wore a crown,
She kissed him,
He turned handsome,
It was true love.

Jayan Patel (11)
Tudor Primary School

MY GRANDMA

My hidden treasure is my grandma
She always love me
Like an angel
But now she gone
My heart has torn

Her eyes are like the stars
As she gazed at me
I love her all my heart
As she says to me
She gives me a lot of food
But not give me a bad mood.

She always take care of me
Even when I have a cut she always cleans my knee
I love my grandma
As she loves me
But now she gone to Heaven
I always love her.

Randeep Chana (11)
Tudor Primary School

FRUITS

My apple's so crunchy to eat and swallow,
My lemon's so bitter to squeeze and squash,
My orange's so juicy, so sweet and fruity,
My grapes are so soft to bite with my teeth,
My melon's so sweet to eat with my teeth.

Davinder Dhanda (8)
Tudor Primary School

MY GRAN USED TO BE A PIRATE

My gran used to be a pirate,
She found lots of treasures,
And kept it for herself with pleasure,
Once she saw some bones on a lake,
She wasn't scared and didn't care,
And then there was a time she saw a piece of pie,
She just went up and said it was mine.
My gran was a pirate,
Who wash her feet,
But never brushed her teeth.

So be afraid because . . .
I'm a pirate who likes to eat lots of cake.

Gurkirat Kaur Rehal (10)
Tudor Primary School

MY TREASURE

I hold in my hands,
A box of gold,
With a secret inside,
That has never been told.

The box is priceless,
But as I see,
The treasure inside,
Is far more precious to me.

Today I share,
This treasure with thee,
It's the treasure of friendship,
You've given to me!

Omar Abdalle (11)
Tudor Primary School

MY HOLIDAY

We left for Spain
For our summer holiday
It was the first time I'd been on a plane.

The thrill of it all
Gazing out of the window
Were the clouds
Which just looked like cotton wool.

We had to wait for our car
Which made me so bored
When we got in our car
The journey was so far.

When I got there
I had something to eat
While my mum and dad unpacked
I just sat and rested my feet.

The next morning it was nice and sunny
My sister was still playing with her doll
And my brother made me laugh
Because he was so funny.

There were cats that always went by
We always had to feed them
But when you looked up
There was a bright blue sky.

I went swimming in the pool
I had a great time
My brother and sister and I
Thought Spain was so cool.

Holly Craft (10)
Weald Middle School

A WONDERFUL PLANET

Billions of years ago,
In a vast, empty space,
A planet was born,
That would hold the human race.

It started as gas,
And bits of dust,
Then the surface cooled,
To form a hard crust.

The crust was covered,
In volcanoes and craters,
But that all happened,
Millions of years later.

The planet cooled further,
And out from the steam,
Came rivers and oceans,
Lakes and some streams.

This whole process,
Was the birth,
Of a wonderful planet,
We call 'Earth'.

Hannah Pinchen (10)
Weald Middle School

WHEN I WAS YOUNG

When I was young I had no sense,
I pulled my brother over the fence.
I gave him a kick,
It made him sick.
I gave him a smack,
And he fell back.

I said, 'Sorry,'
And went in the lorry.
I gave him a whack,
And then he went back.
And then I went home,
And left him alone.

Monic O'Callaghan (9)
Weald Middle School

THE LION

The lion is gold,
It makes it look bold.

The lion has sharp claws,
And also big paws.

He is the king of the jungle,
He is the king of the jungle.

He runs like lightning,
He's so frightening.

He is the king of the jungle,
He is the king of the jungle.

He is a golden statue,
Until he's ready to catch you.

He's like a giant cat,
Who's golden and that's that.

He is the king of the jungle,
He is the king of the jungle.

David Harrison (10)
Weald Middle School

METAL BIRDS

They fly high up in the sky
With clouds and birds passing by

Taking people lots of places
On holiday with smiling faces

Some planes are used for war
Fast and furious they soar

Finding targets down below
Dropping bombs that blast and blow

With engines making a roaring sound
And wings that stand out long and proud

I really like these metal birds
That help us travel around all the world.

Haden Cummins (10)
Weald Middle School

WHAT WOULD I FIND IN A TEENAGE WITCH'S POCKET IN 3005?

I would find a teleporting remote that can kill children
And a little button that changes her into any person.
A broom called 3200, along, superficial wand,
A magic communication phone,
A flying carpet that sings Destiny Child's albums
And a pack of Wotsits that never ends
And if you say something
And put your hand in the pack of Wotsits
It will come out.

Bhavik J Shah (9)
Weald Middle School

POLAR BEARS

Polar bears' fur is as white like snow,
All its hair standing in a row!

Its eyes are like the night,
Oh look, they're so bright.

Polar bears eat seals,
Theirs is a big meal.

When they sleep,
They don't open their eyes one peep.

Every morning they jump into the sea,
And circle round for their morning tea.

Polar bears live in cold places,
And keep away from stale spaces.

The cubs are white and shining bright,
They're so soft, I'm happy with delight.

Leanna Hagyard (9)
Weald Middle School

A LITTLE SHORT AND SWEET RABBIT POEM

Rabbits are so fair
And love to be rare.

Hiding in grass
And loves to prance.

Sitting in the corner with Little Jack Horner
While sticking their thumb in hot, hot plum.

Amy Backda (10)
Weald Middle School

IN MY BEDROOM

In my bedroom,
I have a wardrobe,
And in my wardrobe,
I have . . .

Ten spiders crawling around,
Nine ants that crawl up my sleeve,
Eight barking dogs,
Seven running hamsters,
Six lazy pigs,
Five black cats,
Four white mice,
Three slithering snails,
Two hopping rabbits,
And,
One slithering slug!

Katie Holroyd (10)
Weald Middle School

JAKE'S CAKE

There was a boy called Jake
Who lived by the lake
He baked a cake that looked fake
His best mate dropped the cake
For goodness sake!
I'll have to bake another cake
This time the cake did not look fake
But it made Jake's stomach ache!
The next morning he wakes up with temptation
To eat the leftover cake.

Huzefa Sam (8)
Weald Middle School

FAMOUS PEOPLE

Each peach, pear, plum
I see Tom Thumb.
Tom Thumb in the wood
Look, there is Robin Hood.
Robin Hood in the cellar,
There is glamorous Cinderella.
Cinderella on a plane
Looks like she's going to Spain.
Jackie Chan went to France
To beat up his great aunts.
Jackie Chan went to jail
In the stomach of the whale.
The whale sneezed,
Out came Jackie,
Back home, he's so happy.
Where's that Cinderella girl?
Looks like she's hiding behind her curl.

Mafaal Faal-Mason (9)
Weald Middle School

THE WHISPERING TREE

Down in the deep, black wood,
There stood a lonely tree,
Not an oak, not a grape or a banana,
Just an ordinary tree.

So down in the dark wood,
How old was that tree?
Some say it's one, some say it's two,
But I say it's three because it whispers at me!

Charlotte Preston (9)
Weald Middle School

ORANG-UTANS IN BORNEO

Swinging in the trees and swallowing bugs,
Swerving round corners goes Dr Orang;

He likes munching on the figs,
So high, up in the trees twigs;

When danger comes he is shy,
So he hides in the trees so high;

Orangs make nests in the trees,
To keep out intruders they pile leaves;

His fur is the colour of autumn orange,
And his arms very, very long;

His coconut-coloured eyes are so bright,
Every day and night they reflect the light;

Mr Orang's final line is 'Nunight,
You see my eyes glowing every day,
But now I'm putting them away!'

Daniel Mullick (10)
Weald Middle School

SNAKE

A snake is as long as a bus
    It will eat a human without a fuss

He is like a killing machine and not very clean
    He is human-eating, mouse-beating snake

He likes flesh and making a mess
    And, worst of all, he couldn't care less.

Dominic Ansell (9)
Weald Middle School

PENGUIN

A penguin is nice and cute
And I don't think that's a fluke

A penguin can have a good swim
And walks with a kind of limp

A penguin wobbles like jelly
And is sometimes very smelly

A penguin eats a lot of fish
But never quite on a dish

A penguin is a sapling because it's so short
Its favourite car is Ford Escort

I think the penguin is the best
So much better than the rest.

Alex O'Brien (9)
Weald Middle School

WHY?

Why do people get sad?
   Why do people get mad?
Why do people bully?
   Why do people moan?
Why do people groan?
   Why is the world round?
Why do we walk on ground?
   Why do people cry?
Why do people shy?
   Why is some of the world rich?
Why is some of the world poor?
   We would like to know the answers.

Mary Ademoye (9)
Weald Middle School

MY DREAMS, NIGHTMARES AND WISHES

My dream is to fly up high,
Soaring through the bright blue sky.
My nightmare is to be alone,
Without a friend, without a home.
My dream is to swim under sea,
In the deep ocean is where you'll find me.
My nightmare is for a broken heart,
To be left alone, cold in the dark.
My dream is to go into space,
Onto a planet without a trace.
My nightmare is to be afraid,
With no one there to guide the way.
My wish is for my dreams to stay,
For my bad dreams to go away.

My best dream would be:

To be a singer,
To be a bell ringer,
To be a teacher,
To be a star reacher.

Lauren Dale (9)
Weald Middle School

MY FAMILY

My mum has a big bottom,
Her jacket has big button,
She walks to work every day
And comes home and says, 'Hooray!'

My dad is always grumpy
And always is jumpy.
He plays around
And has no pounds.

My brother thinks of his girlfriend
And always bends my head.
His best friend is dumb
Because he has a big tum!

Misha Upadhyaya (10)
Weald Middle School

MUMS AND DADS

My mum is one of the cuddliest mums in town
She's the best, I love her and hate it when she's down
My mum, otherwise known as Dee, fills me with glee
And when she's mad she always feels sorry for me.

Dads are a different matter, they never shout and scream
And when you're in bed at night he's there if you have a bad dream
My dad was a delivery man and drove a delivery van
He would never drop litter or ever kick a can.

Joe, my brother is an annoying little brat
He loves our pets, Charlie and Speedie, the cats
Me and Joe always love a fight
But we never scare each other at night.

Grandad is in the country with his dog
All the way in the country with logs
I like his trousers and jumpers too
He likes his food and doesn't take long to chew.

Grandma is cool and takes me swimming
She's a teacher and works with lots of women
I love my grandma, she's ten out of ten
So that's my favourite family. The end.

Nadine Coton (9)
Weald Middle School

MONKEY AND A MOTHER

Living in a large, caring family
In a green, leafy place
With lots of trees
It's hot and relaxing and great
When you were born a little baby
With a nice, pink face
When you grow up
Your body will be covered by a long, soft, black hair
It looks so nice on you
And you will be fresh, new
When you have tiny hands, face and feet
You cling to your mother's tummy
And make her food yummy!
You spend seven hours eating delicious, yummy, mainly fruit
And also some of your favourite food is a snack of ants
If you are thirsty you go to the river and drink
It is hard to reach a leaf to make quite, sound, soft, nice, fantastic,
                                          great, relaxing voices
Climbing tree is free
I grow up and be good and strong, bravey and behivy.

Islam Elamin (12)
Weald Middle School

THE PEANUT

There was a peanut who was alive
There was a peanut who could not dive
There was a peanut who could not count up to five
There was a peanut who could not have a wife
There was a peanut who could not hold a knife
There was a peanut who got eaten alive.

Yasin Ali (9)
Weald Middle School

TEN THINGS IN MY TEACHER'S POCKET

I was sitting in my class one day,
When my teacher stopped and looked my way.
'I need your help, if you please,
I think that I have lost my keys.
My lunch is in my desk and I have locked it.'
Please can you look in my pocket?'
But I did not find her keys,
All I found where these:
A mini TV for her to watch,
A computer to plan her work,
A Harry Potter book for her to read,
A piece of chalk for her to write with,
A bottle of purple nail varnish,
A packet of sweets for her treat,
Stickers for her to give to the class,
A calculator to do her sums,
And a CD of her favourite songs
But no keys!

Romy Cummins (8)
Weald Middle School

THE MOTHER NATURE POEM

You are the fairy who makes the flowers bloom.
You are the fairy who makes the wind blow in my face.
You are the fairy who makes rain that falls on my head.
You are the fairy of all things little and big.
You are the fairy who makes the sun shine bright.
You are the fairy who puts a rainbow in the sky.
You are the fairy of all things.
You are the one and only Mother Nature.

Talar Bourne (8)
Weald Middle School

PEACE

I wish there was no war,
For people who are poor.
I wish there was no pollution,
In any situation.
I wish there was no murder,
For people who don't surrender.
I wish there was no killing,
This is *worldwide appealing!*
What's wrong with peace and kindness?
We like to see happiness.
This must be the job for the police,
To store law and order in *peace.*
It's not fair to those who have died,
Justice must be done worldwide.
No excuse for anyone,
Rich, powerful and those with none.
Short, medium or tall,
Peace is our mission for all.
Let's get together and shout,
'If you don't like it just get out!'

Nasim Nayeri (10)
Weald Middle School

THE MOON

The moon is round,
The moon is bright,
The moon shines on us
All through the night.

Sometimes half,
Sometimes full,
And the moon will
Shine upon us all.

The moon is round,
The moon is bright,
The moon shines on us
All through the night.

When the morning comes,
There's no moon in sight,
The sun shines through my window,
It must be the end of the night.

Charlotte Morgan (9)
Weald Middle School

MY HOUSE

When I wake up every day
All I see is this:
Dustbin can
A really old man
And the rest of Hillbilly Road
But most of all you see no more
Is the house that we live in.

A bucket of pie
A chicken Kiev
Of course is what I eat
When my mum says,
'Homework time,'
She groaned and walked away.

When you see our disgraceful street
You will wonder what we do
Hillbilly Street is a mad street
And mad is what we are.

Leila Kay Thurgar (10)
Weald Middle School

THE ALIENS

They aliens have landed
They are stranded
On a beautiful island
They've named it
Sintoki Griland
They're looking for food
And they're in a bad mood
They can't eat meat
And they don't like heat
They've lost all transmissions
And they're on a rescue mission
Whatever shall they do?
New aliens have landed
To take home those that were stranded.

'Hallelujah!' they cry.

Zoë Veary (9)
Weald Middle School

PROBLEM?

Firm holder
Tennis player
Ball murderer
Vicious slayer
Fast runner
Grass champion
Tennis cracker
Tennis whacker
And an enormously
Fast server
Can you guess who it is?

Karan Joshi (10)
Weald Middle School

FISH

'I wish, I wish I were a fish,'
Said Bobby to his sister
As in his net, he chanced to get
A little, speckled twister.

I wish, I wish I were a fish
With all my dear relations
no need to go to school, you know
And never do dictations
And never have to wash or dress
And never to be beaten.

'Quite so,' the fish remarked,
'Unless you happen to be eaten!'

Mohammad Datoo (10)
Weald Middle School

THE SEA

The sea is blue.
The sea is calm.
It's like a shiny, precious charm.
The waves are curly like a pig's tail.
Boats row on the deep blue sea.
When you float you bob up and down
And water laps around your hands and feet.
When you get out of the great, huge pool
Your feet sink into the sandy beach.
Seaweed wraps around your feet
And then you walk home in the sunset.

Amy J Smith (9)
Weald Middle School

CHRISTMAS

It's nearly Christmas
I just can't wait
I'll get lots of presents
It's going to be great!

I'll put up some tinsel here and there
Hey! She's got more presents than me
It's just not fair!

'Let's decorate the tree,'
I shouted with glee
And hung the chocolate onto the tree.

Now I hang up my stockings one by one
Waiting for Santa to fill on Christmas Eve.

Karina Thakrar (10)
Weald Middle School

BELLS

The bell in the clock
That stands on the self,
Slowly, sleepily
Talks to itself.

The school bell is noisy,
And bangs like brass.
Hurry up! Hurry up!
Late for lesson,
Late for class.

Murtuza Qayoom (9)
Weald Middle School

HAMMERHEAD SHARK

As big as a car,
And could eat a steel bar.

Is so strong,
Never wrong.

Is a killing machine,
And not very clean.

Eyes like a hawk,
Eats people that walk.

It moves so fast,
Like a rocket blast.

It will give you a bite,
In the darkness of the night.

It will beat you,
And eat you.

Elliott Frame (9)
Weald Middle School